HISTORY BY DESIGN:
A PRIMER ON INTERPRETING AND
EXHIBITING COMMUNITY HISTORY

HISTORY
BY
DESIGN:

☒

A PRIMER ON INTERPRETING
AND EXHIBITING
COMMUNITY HISTORY

by
Patrick Norris

◪

TEXAS ASSOCIATION OF MUSEUMS
Austin, Texas

Copyright © 1985

Texas Association of Museums
P.O. Box 13353
Austin, Texas 78711

ISBN 0–935260–02–1

Publication of this book was made possible in part by
funds from the Texas Committee for the Humanities.

Design by Barbara Jezek

Typography by G & S Typesetters, Inc., Austin, Texas

Printed by The Whitley Company, Austin, Texas

The cover design motif was adapted from the hinges
on the doors of The Texas State Capitol, Austin.

*DEDICATED
TO THE MEMORY OF
GLENDA G. MORGAN*

THE INTEGRITY
OF THE ARTIFACT

Conservation is an attempt to prolong the life of objects of historical and artistic value. The primary job of saving them can be done through providing proper safeguards for the objects against environmental extremes: such as strong light, humidity and temperature fluctuations; insects, animals, and micro-organisms; vandalism or burglary and curatorial ignorance or carelessness—the ravages of man.

The important part of conservation, like medicine, is prevention rather than cure. An unskilled enthusiast who undertakes to clean and repair an object often lacks an understanding of materials and methods. In his zeal he usually does too much rather than too little, and sometimes does irreparable damage. It is important never to do anything that you do not completely understand. Restraint and skill go hand-in-hand.

Neither traditional techniques nor modern discoveries will extend the life of an object half as much as primary conservation—that is, proper care and maintenance of the objects in one's possession. We are only temporary custodians of antiquities, and it is our responsibility to see that they are passed on to the future.

Excerpted from: Per E. Guldbeck, *The Care of Historical Collections: A Conservation Handbook for the Nonspecialist* (Nashville, TN: American Association for State and Local History, 1972). pp 1–2.

Contents

Preface

❖·❖·❖

In the spring of 1983, the Texas Association of Museums with the assistance of the Texas Historical Commission, sponsored a regional workshop series, "Presenting the Past: Researching and Interpreting Your Community's History," in eight communities around the state. Funding was provided by the Texas Committee for the Humanities. Additional support for this publication was received from the Fort Worth Museum of Science and History, Fort Worth, Texas, and from the Institute of Museum Services, Washington, D.C.

The workshops brought a faculty of six historians, curators, and museum directors together with teachers, librarians, local historians, and museum volunteers. The speakers addressed the nature of community history, the techniques of historical and artifactual analysis, and the design of exhibits. They presented, in turn, a set of basic assumptions about history in general and community history in particular; a sense of the sources that we examine to establish historical facts; and, an understanding of how historical materials, especially artifacts, are arranged into exhibits.

Glenda G. Morgan and Cindy Sherrell-Leo of the Texas Historical Commission and Amanda Stover of the Texas Association of Museums asked me to serve as the Humanities Writer for the workshop. My assignment was to adapt the speakers' comments into a primer for the Texas Sesquicentennial. This essay is the result.

I owe a primary debt to the six speakers whose comments provided a basic text. I have tried to faithfully present the substance, and where possible, to preserve the tone of their remarks. I worked from tapes and transcripts of their presentations, and, in several instances, faced the additional problem of reworking what were originally slide presentations. I have, therefore, supplemented their ideas with my own perspectives and those of our colleagues.

Don Carleton, Director of the Barker Texas History Center, U.T. Austin, outlined the philosophy of history that is elaborated in the opening chapter. Two curators and historians, Ron Tyler of the Amon Carter Museum, Fort Worth, and Patrick H. Butler of the Harris County Heritage Society, Houston, described the tasks of research that are discussed in the second chapter. Conover Hunt, formerly Chief Curator at the Dallas Historical Society and now an independent consultant, explored the uses of artifacts, the unwritten materials of history, that are analyzed in the third chapter. Sam Hoyle, Director of the U.S. Army Air Defense Artillery Museum, Fort Bliss, and David Ross, Director of the McAllen International Museum, explained how the sources of history written and unwritten, can be artfully arranged into exhibits, the subject of the fourth chapter. Patrick H. Butler also contributed the appendix, "Resources for Texas History," which lists archives, museums, and regional historical depositories.

I am grateful for the speakers' comments on the first draft of this text and for the careful reading that members of the TAM Publications Committee gave to it. I especially appreciate the time that Patty Harrington and Donna Jones spent reading the first draft, that Samuel Moore Hudson gave to helping me edit it, and that Diana Getchell spent typing several versions.

On behalf of the Council of the Texas Association of Museums, I am pleased to dedicate this book to the memory of my friend and colleague, Glenda G. Morgan, who served the cause of Texas community history for thirteen years as a museum director and consultant. Glenda's warmth and good humor, her advice and counsel, touched us all.

Patrick Norris

Introduction

GETTING A FIRM GRIP
ON THE OBVIOUS

This book introduces the tasks and tools of community history. It is written with two underlying assumptions: that Texas is a fascinating part of the world; and, that within Texas communities there are and were people, places, and events infinitely worth serious (if not always solemn) attention, and informed, honest storytelling.

The Texas Sesquicentennial provides an opportunity to explore how our communities have come to be and to understand who we are and why. Discovering, creating, and telling community history requires hard work, long thought, a willingness to be surprised, and a keen eye for the facts. Don Carleton, Director of the Barker Texas History Center, expressed the challenge of community history as "getting a firm grip on the obvious."

The history of Texas communities compels our interest because it is obvious. It lies all around us, everyday. Its subject is our immediate environment, and the places, people, objects, and events that shaped our environment. Because these subjects are so close to us, they are also elusive. Great events and great men are chronicled, studied, debated from varying points of view. The things of everyday life and the lives of ordinary people too often pass by unsung.

Walt Whitman was right: "the United States themselves are essentially the greatest poem." That greatness resides in the lives of their people. When we celebrate 150 years of Texas, let us sing the verses that Texans have written in Texas communities.

1

THINKING
HISTORICALLY

⊠

A portion of the material presented in Chapter One was developed for the workshops by Don Carleton, Director of the Barker Texas History Center, U.T. Austin.

Chapter 1:

THINKING HISTORICALLY

W HEN YOU USE THE PAST TENSE in everyday conversation, when you read a newspaper, write a letter, retell a favorite story at the dinner table, keep a diary or make a photograph, you are practicing history. In the words of historian Carl Becker, you are "creating a memory of things said or done."

Becker's definition reduces history to two essential elements. "Things said or done" are the actual events of the past, the facts of history. "Memory" is our present understanding of what has taken place, of what the facts mean. History is the relationship between what has happened—events—and what we understand events to mean—their significance.

We intertwine past and present in almost everything we do—in our daily living, in our beliefs and passions, and in the institutions that reflect and sustain us. History, in short, is one of the basic ways in which we think. In making sense out of the present by relating it to the past, every man is, as Becker entitled the essay from which his definition is taken, his own historian.

We have been told that History teaches this or that, and that those who do not understand History are condemned to repeat it. These statements suggest that history is an abstraction, that it exists apart form and prior to us, and that it is absolute and unchanging.

Certainly, historical events exist independent of human recollection. From time to time, new evidence brings to light events that change our understanding of the past. History does have an objective side. Determining what was said and done depends ultimately on analyzing the available evidence. New evidence can alter interpretation, reshape memory, re-create history. But facts alone are mute. What they mean depends on how they are interpreted, that is, made to speak.

History has a second side, the subjective component that Becker labels memory. To the evidence of things said and done, historians bring their values, assumptions, interests, and techniques. They add a critical and analytical point of view that gives meaning to mute facts. Historians select and arrange facts to explain what happened. They say what the facts mean. They speak through the discipline of facts.

History is, thus, the product of men and women who put facts in order and create interpretations of those facts. Becker's definition (and ours) underscores the fact that *people* write history. History changes as values, interests, and needs change. History is rewritten (1) because new facts come to light; (2) because new ways of assembling and understanding those facts arise; (3) because new questions are suggested by the reinterpretation of new materials, and, (4) because every age has new problems to understand.

By itself, history teaches us nothing; those who practice history teach us. Historians critically analyze the past to help us understand the nature and values of the society in which we live: they illuminate our origins. They also influence our response to the problems that confront us: they clarify our choices.

When we think historically, we engage in a three-stage process. First, we establish what was said or done; we investigate the evidence to uncover the facts of history. This is what we call research, and it is the subject of the next chapter. Second, we interpret the facts to ascertain the pattern and the meaning of what was said and done. Interpretation requires judgment, based on our research *and* on our values, needs, and interests. Interpretation is the focus of our third chapter. We communicate the results of our research and our interpretation. How we can write history through exhibits is the topic of our final chapter.

The Role of Local History

Within this framework, local history is both one of the least developed and one of the most important forms of history. Far too often, local histories were long on details and short on interpretation. They were lists of events, chronicles; or family trees, genealogies; or compilations of facts, records. But because they failed to follow through by giving meaning to things once said and done, they were not history.

Scholars used to dismiss these forms of local history as "history with the brains left out." Their complaint was that the conventional approach massed facts but did not select and order them. This concern with details for the sake of detail is called antiquarianism. Antiquarianism robs history of the meaning interpretation gives. Filiopiety, the uncritical celebration of the town's founders, leading citizens, and their accomplishments compounds the disorder of antiquarianism. A sad result was history written to a familiar theme—the March of Progress!—and written with a conventional formula that began with a romantic view of Native Americans; recounted the trials of the first settlers; chronicled a series of "Firsts," milestones in government and economic development; and then concluded with a nostalgic essay interspersed with photographs of The Good Old Days.

In recent years, local history has begun to come into its own. Interest in topics of local significance responds to a genuine need for a sense of who we Americans are. Our quest for self-identity has been expressed in the popularity of family history, in the development of a historic preservation movement, and in celebrations of the Bicentennial. These activities reflect an effort to place one's family, or immediate environment, or hometown into a historical framework. Genealogy personalizes a sense of time, just as rescuing and restoring architecturally significant structures creates a sense of place. And in events that marked the nation's beginnings, communities were exploring and renewing their own sense of place and time. Future historians may explain the popularity of local history as a response to the pressures of our own time, expressing disillusionment over failures in Viet Nam and Watergate or mirroring a general modern feeling of rootlessness and lost identity. However caused, this interest comes from the grass roots and reflects the importance that people attach to their local communities.

Professional historians have also renewed their concern for topics of local history during the last twenty years. They have accepted the view that an understanding of community history is necessary to explain the forces that shape our national experience. They treat local events as prisms through which broader trends can be focused. The impulse to look seriously at communities has expressed itself in two fields of scholarship: social history and urban history.

Proclaiming itself "history from the bottom up," the "new social history" marks a shift toward different topics and different approaches than the older tradition in history which looked at leaders and in social history which emphasized the evolution of style and chronicled changing fashions. Social historians seek to recover the history of ordinary people and everyday experience through traces left in census records, fragmentary writings, landscapes, photographs, and common objects. To read these sources, they are turning to statistical analyses and to other research techniques: artifact and photograph analysis, oral history, and human geography. These methods mark a shift in approach away from elite individuals, high style, and major events per se and toward the processes of change, trends, and group behavior over time.

Social historians investigate topics such as family structure, patterns of land ownership, the effect of economic change on manmade landscapes, social welfare, and educational opportunities. Social historians are producing case studies of particular localities to test theories about the relationships expressed within them. The case study method allows them to isolate and examine closely forces at work in society at large.

Urban historians seek to understand how communities are

formed and develop. They inquire into the historical sources of problems that now afflict city life: crime, pollution, social tensions, inadequate services, poverty, and the like. The case study approach not only fits the locus of their overall concern—the city itself—but it also defines limits for problems under investigation, keeps the scale of research manageable, and builds a framework for comparative analyses. And so large questions like the impact of urbanization on the extent and character of social mobility have been addressed through the cases of Plymouth Colony in 1700, Boston in 1850, Chicago in 1900, or other particular cities at other times.

Both urban history and the new social history look through the prism of the local community to see broader questions. They have paved the way for other historians in the imaginative use of sources. From their work, regardless of the time or place studied, you will find ways to understand the history of Texas communities. Their approaches hold promise that a unified understanding of American local history may emerge in the future. For the present, their work suggests some guidelines essential to the practice of local history for its own sake.

GUIDELINE NO. 1

Place Your Subject Into a Context

Local communities are organisms that constantly adapt to pressures from their external environment. The relationship between a locality and its surrounding communities—religions, states, the nation itself—can be conceived as a series of concentric circles. Each, British historian H. P. R. Finberg has written, must be understood "with constant reference to the one outside it." Just as social and urban historians have focused on their concerns through the study of specific communities, you should look outward to the forces that impinge on your subject. This requires a sense of historical context that comes from wide background reading. Try to establish a dialogue between the unique and the general. Precede your research with general reading in history of your region, the state, and the nation at large. Some sources for Texas history will be mentioned in the next chapter.

Local historians should be familiar with the meaning and character of the processes that have been the subjects of academic inquiry: modernization, settlement, industrialization, and other changes in the ways people do things. You should also be prepared to examine the cases of other local communities in the state and region for insight into particular responses to these general trends. Reading through the concentric circles will establish an appreciation for genuine similarities and differences in a specific community's past and make you sensitive to the broader significance of events.

GUIDELINE NO. 2

Develop an Interpretive Framework

Building a sense of context will reveal concepts which can define those aspects of a community's past that are significant enough for further investigation. Without some way to order your evidence, some conceptual scaffolding, local history remains a mass of data, a catalog of names, dates, and events. The different meanings of the word "community" will help you see how an interpretive framework can help sort facts.

Community, first of all, describes a particular place. One question that must be addressed is why that place was created. For those parts of Texas that were settled in the 1830's, local historians need to understand the values and motivations of Jacksonian America, a nation whose attention centered on economic opportunities. People who founded communities like Houston were town promoters, real estate hustlers, urban speculators who came here to buy land, parcel it, and, above all, make money in the bargain. Land developers settled Texas then, and have shaped its geography ever since. Once selected, the characteristics of a particular place—its landscape, climate, topography—further shaped choices and opportunities. And so developing a lively sense of place can be one key to unlocking your community's past.

Secondly, community describes the network of personal relationships that develop within a particular place. Occupational categories, ethnic minorities, fraternal organizations, congregations, neighborhoods, family and kinship groups are communities, in this sense. Because people conceive of themselves as members of different groups, group interplay makes up a great part of a community's past. You thus face an obligation to deal with all of the groups that have comprised your community and with all of the people who comprised those groups.

Thomas Carlyle defined history as the biography of great men. Conventional local histories used to tell only the story of pioneers and of prominent families who dominated the community. They missed the rich detail and complexity in the real story. The whole community includes laborers and merchants, women and children, blacks and whites and Hispanics. As a local historian, you will need to respect and represent this range of experience and explain as many levels of community life as you can.

In a third sense, the word community refers to an intangible quality, a sense of shared intimacy, of belonging and identity experienced by people inhabiting a specific place. Urban historians have identified the decline of community as a feature of the transition from the autonomous local units of the Nineteenth Century into the integrated mass society of today. How modernization has in fact affected the sense of community—whether it has declined or persists, whether it remains in the community at large—provides another interpretive handle that uses all three meanings of the word.

The meanings of the word community provide three assumptions that can guide your interpretation of your town: (1) that its location and environment determined available choices and shaped experience; (2) that its people organized themselves into groups and that, together, these comprised its unity; and, (3) that a sense of self-identity developed out of place and shared experience. Each and every town has a story of its own to tell, a life history that contains the hopes and struggles, dreams and successes of the people who have made its history. This story is significant *in its own right*, not simply as an example of general processes like modernization. Important as it is to identify common patterns of urban development and general trends in social history, focusing solely on these obscures the variety and detail of individual experiences; it illuminates the big picture at the price of missing what actually happened to ordinary people in real towns.

Three other questions can take you to the heart of what actually happened: What was it like then? How has it changed? Why is it different? The first question asks you to describe the past, to take a slice of time and explore themes defined within it, perhaps a single neighborhood or activity or incident. The second question requires you to measure change over time, to cover the sweep of events and to focus on the sequence of their unfolding. With the third question, you inquire into causes and consequences, into the influence of various factors and the logic of their relations. The answers will begin to build your interpretive framework. There is no single, best approach to community history. Different focuses yield different results. It is just as valid to center your research on an intense examination of one theme as it is to cover the entire history of a community.

GUIDELINE NO. 3

Deal with Conflict

Regardless of the questions you ask or the approach you take, remember that conflicts reveal a community's inner dynamics. Just as it is necessary to deal with all the people who make up the community, it is vital to understand the full character of its life. If we interpret only happy occasions, we will be ignoring half the truth and almost all of the excitement. People express their values openly, often dramatically, and always most frankly when caught up in conflicts that involve religion, race, politics, and choices both public and private. Nice or not, such conflicts are the very heart and soul of much of our group life. Moreover, conflicts make for a good story; they infuse drama and create interest in apparently ordinary events. And conflicts tell us a lot about ourselves. Behind a hotly contested election for the school board lies a great deal of information about how people feel about education or taxation, about a community's social and economic structure, and about its pride and its view of the future.

Because your audience is the entire community, conflicts are often difficult to discuss. You risk offending one group or another, and you will meet critics of your work at the supermarket, in church, or on the street. Your local public can be a real constraint on your willingness to tell the whole story. But this is a constraint that you consciously will have to fight against. Conflicts are a fact of all life and important to history; and you must work within the discipline of the facts. There is no sure way to solve this problem, but the rewards for risks you take may be significant. By presenting all sides of a conflict, fully and faithfully, you establish contact across what divides and separates people, and you may change the way they regard each other and themselves.

GUIDELINE NO. 4

Discuss the Twentieth Century

Local histories used to deal only with the beginnings of the community, with the first two generations: the pioneers and the town builders. The temptations to redo early history are many. For one, the subject is safe. Pioneers are long dead; their characters and deeds have taken on a mythic quality. They seem larger than life as we know it. They struggled and suffered more than we do. They believed more firmly than we do. They accomplished more than we have. They are the subjects we recall in television and motion pictures. And their history seems more interesting. Secondly, it is easier to reheat old history than it is to create it from scratch. Early history seems more manageable; its sources can be more easily mastered; less of the raw data survives, and what has survived is recorded and readily accessible. The very lack of detail tempts us to tell again only the beginning of the story.

But to try to write a history of the Twentieth Century is the task that challenges us now. We must begin the process of helping people understand their own times by tracing the ways in which great events and changes have worked themselves out in local contexts. There are many ways to approach our times. You can draw a contrast between the work of an average housewife in 1900 and today. The automobile redrew the face of Texas. It ended island communities; it shaped and continues to shape the pace and structure of life. If you choose significant, but limited topics like these, your task as a local historian becomes more "do-able" than it might seem at first, but no less important.

Much Texas history was made in the Twentieth Century. You should seriously consider focusing your Sesquicentennial attention on the last eighty years in your community. Some communities began only in this century, as did most of the changes that have reshaped our culture: oil, automobiles, airplanes, aerospace. In many ways, Texas began to have a major impact on the rest of the country only after 1900.

GUIDELINE NO. 5

Do Not Overemphasize the Distinctiveness of Your Community

Every town has its unique aspects, its own historical experience; and people take pride in the particular identity of their community. Often, that sense of distinctiveness is summed up in an annual celebration of one dramatic event or feature of the town's past. Gonzales was the Lexington of the Texas Revolution, but it also represents one of the finest instances of

Spanish urban design in colonial America. Its being the place where the first shot was fired for Texas independence has overwhelmed this other, truly distinctive feature of Gonzales' past. It is very tempting for a community historian to fall in with these celebrations of uniqueness and to ignore the rest of the story. Celebrations have clear popular appeal; they are fun, but they often perpetuate the myths of history.

But when you explore the Twentieth Century, you have to re-emphasize the theme of interdependence. Our lives as Americans have become much more interconnected than ever before. Whether you live in Houston or Dalhart, Alpine or Dallas, Brownsville or Wichita Falls, you are daily and directly affected by decisions made at the state capital, in Washington or New York, or Hollywood. Nineteenth Century Texas was very different; its towns and cities were economically and culturally autonomous. Ties to the larger society were weaker than they are today. Before the spread of railroads, transportation was much slower and more expensive. Government at all levels was less active, and its authority was little felt in many areas of life. National corporations and national advertising arrived late in the Nineteenth Century.

Life has become much different today and it is inaccurate to portray your community as isolated and utterly distinctive. Even in small rural communities, people live much like urban Americans. They drive pickups and use machinery manufactured and distributed by a mass industrial economy. They wear the same clothes, eat the same food, watch the same television programs, and listen to the same popular music. Indeed, much of their self image as rural people is mass produced and marketed from urban environments. Grass roots historians need to trace the decline of cultural and economic autonomy; this is the process called modernization, and you will need to deal with your part of Texas being modernized, for better or worse.

You should also note and try to discover the ways in which your community has remained different, and how it resembles others in your region and in Texas as a whole. Your background reading will suggest questions that need to be considered. Why, for instance, are so many Texas communities laid out in a grid pattern? Why are their streets numbered in one direction and named after trees in the other? Why do houses resemble each other in community after community? Why did your town and so many towns in Texas establish a fire department and a police force at a certain time in the late Nineteenth Century? Why did towns over and over again have improvement associations which planted boulevard trees and rose bushes? These similarities are not simple coincidences. Seeing these larger patterns and seeing how your community fit into them is a step away from the romantic and inaccurate notion that every community was or can be autonomous.

SUMMARY

Doing Local History

Our discussion has urged a different conception of history and of the local historian's role as its practitioner than is usually assumed. We began by defining history as the memory of things said and done, and we portrayed it as the activity by which we critically analyze the past. That last phrase is crucial. Historians do not simply record the facts in their natural order. There can be no natural order until the historian imposes his own order on things said and done. We identified the process that you will engage in to create memory: a process of investigation, interpretation, and communication. Each of these phases will be explored in the chapters that follow.

We singled out the importance of local history both to the people whose lives and environment it explores and to professional historians who are rediscovering its meaning. The subject of history is much more than great men and wars; it is also the story of the ordinary men and women and everyday life. Before the Twentieth Century, the concerns of most Americans were centered in communities. Local events circumscribed their world. In the Twentieth Century, local communities have been the stages on which great technological and social changes of our time have been played out. Only through understanding that changing reality can we explain the forces that have shaped our national experience and that have ho- mogenized and transformed the character of community life.

All of these considerations place a great deal of emphasis on the personal qualities of the local historian, on your sense of judgment and proportion, and on your sense of how people behave and how communities operate. This means that as a working community historian, you must be thoroughly in- volved in the concerns of your town *today*. Learn about the range of religious, ethnic, and social groups active in your community and about the conflicts that shape its current his- tory. By being alive to the life around you, you will become aware of the ways in which your community functions and you will gain a perspective on how it always has been special. Your contribution is important not only to a local audience but to all of us who believe that the true history of America is embodied in the lives and local history of its communities.

2

·

THINGS SAID
AND DONE

☒

A portion of the material presented in Chapter Two was developed for the workshops by Ron Tyler of the Amon Carter Museum and Patrick Butler of the Harris County Heritage Society.

Chapter 2:

THINGS SAID AND DONE

WHEN CARL BECKER DEFINED HISTORY as the memory of things said and done, he expressed the idea that every generation inevitably understands the past in light of its own experience. Our understanding of Texas is restricted by commonly accepted interpretations of its history and by the sources that have been researched to create those interpretations. Over the years, new source material surfaces to reshape our understanding. Some fills gaps in our knowledge. Other material causes us to rethink existing interpretations. Although the general outline of Texas history is established by chronology, our views of chapters within that chronology are open to change.

The Barker Texas History Center at the University of Texas has come across an enormous collection of material on antebellum Southern life, a collection that dwarfs most of the known manuscript material on slavery and one that no scholar has seen. A find of this magnitude opens questions that we have long considered resolved. We also are expanding our vision of the father of Texas, Stephen F. Austin, through *Papers Concerning Robertson's Colony in Texas*, a series edited by Malcolm D. McLean and published by the University of Texas at Arlington.

The Life of Stephen F. Austin: Founder of Texas, Eugene C. Barker's the standard biography, devotes a chapter to the Austin-Robertson feud. Now we have another side to the story, and it is challenging the received interpretation in significant ways. Other caches awaiting discovery will cast new light on the "settled" questions.

The discovery of new materials teaches us a fundamental

lesson of historical research—that the data determines the interpretation. New sources reveal facts which can change our understanding by leading us to a more careful analysis of older sources. The point is, first of all, do your research; do not think that all the significant facts have been uncovered. Secondly, do not assume that all the major questions have been resolved. If your research deviates from the accepted interpretation, give it a chance to speak to you. Do not dismiss it simply because it disagrees with received wisdom. Remember Barbara Tuchman's advice: historians speak through the discipline of the facts, new and old.

You find the facts of history through the traces that things said and done leave behind, through what historians call sources. Sources can be divided by type into (1) literary, i.e., written records; (2) non-literary records, maps, drawings, paintings, photographs; (3) artifacts, manmade objects; and, (4) the landscape itself. Historians also divide sources into primary and secondary and tertiary depending on their relation to an event. Primary sources were produced by the event itself; secondary evidence was created soon after; tertiary evidence was produced after analyzing the other evidence. A map used to conduct a battle is a primary source. A soldier's account of his actions in the same battle is secondary evidence. A historian's reconstruction of the battle would be tertiary evidence. Each type and level of source will speak to us once we learn how to listen.

What are useful sources for Texas history? How can they be read? In creating local history, you have a responsibility to present a rounded interpretation, one that can be built only by combining written and unwritten, primary and secondary materials. Exhibits, by their nature, combine a variety of materials and so you have a practical motive for learning how to read all available sources. You have an opportunity to speak through exhibits to the general public, an audience that may not read history in books. You can have an impact; you can reach people who may not have access to other information or time to study it.

Published Sources

This survey of resources for Texas local history will begin with the most accessible: the wide range of published studies that are generally useful for understanding Texas history. Many are secondary or tertiary sources, interpretations that help establish a sense of context, lead to research topics, and provide the basis for comparing one local community to another.

To gain a foothold in Texas history, read these two short books which offer different perspectives on its overall character. D. W. Meinig's *Imperial Texas: An Interpretive Essay in Cultural Geography* (University of Texas Press, 1969) discusses the land itself and the patterns of settlement that have shaped it. T. R. Fehrenbach's *Seven Keys to Texas* (Texas Western Press, 1983) isolates the elements that have gone into the particular chemistry of Texas.

For a deeper understanding of the events and people who shaped Texas, Seymour V. Conner's *Texas: A History* (Thomas Y. Crowell, 1971) and Rupert N. Richardson's *Texas: The Lone Star State*, Third Edition (Prentice-Hall, Inc., 1970) are considered among the best, well written, and balanced accounts. Also useful is Donald W. Whisenhunt's *Texas: A Sesquicentennial Celebration* (Eakin Press, 1984), a collection of new essays by twenty scholars of Texas who have re-evaluated traditional themes in its history.

Among the wide variety of local studies, Randolph B. Campbell's newly published, *A Southern Community in Crisis: Harrison County, Texas, 1850–1880* (Texas State Historical Association/Texas A & M University Press, 1983) is a model of recent historiography. David G. McComb's *Houston: A History* (University of Texas Press, 1981) is an urban biography that has been revised and published in paperback.

The Handbook of Texas (Texas State Historical Association, 1952; Supplement, 1976) is a three-volume encyclopedia with entries on the people, places, and events significant in the development of the state. Since 1897, the publication of the Texas State Historical Association, *Southwestern Historical Quarterly*, has contained articles on every conceivable aspect of Texas history, as well as reviews of newly published works. The articles collected and published as the Texas Folklore Series by Southern Methodist University Press also provide very valuable insights into life in Texas.

John H. Jenkins' *Basic Texas Books: An Annotated Bibliography of Selected Works for a Research Library* (Jenkins Publishing Company, 1983) surveys published Texana. Jenkins focuses on 224 essential books with complete descriptions of their contents and their contribution to the historical literature; he also discusses over a thousand others and includes an annotated guide to 217 Texas bibliographies. Together, these sources can establish a sense of context for you and help you understand the character of Texas history.

What about the artifacts that have shaped and reflect Texas experience? In the next chapter, we will talk about reading artifacts as historical sources and using them as interpretive materials. For now, we will suggest some works that can deepen your understanding of how objects were made, used, and influenced Texas history and American culture. The single most valuable general source for Nineteenth Century objects is the first woman's magazine in America, *Godey's Ladies Book*, which was published in Philadephia beginning in 1838. Predecessor to the modern woman's magazine, *Godey's* set the style for the day; it included popular fiction, piano music, sketches for room arrangements and window treatments, fashion notes, and descriptions of crafts that offer insight into middle class domestic life. It is now available on microfilm in many libraries, and historians have documented its use in Texas. For instance, we know which Godey's window pattern was used to make curtains for the Samuel May Williams house in Galveston.

For the late Nineteenth and early Twentieth Century, *The Sears, Roebuck Catalog* is the best single source of information on Texas material culture. Beginning in 1895, Sears wrought a revolution in merchandising and Texans were major consumers of Sears products. By 1900, Texas accounted for 15% of the national sales of Sears Roebuck. In fact, Texas was the only state to have its own catalog twice a year; between 1906 and 1940, Sears published a special Texas catalog. The early Texas issues have a trilingual introduction: English, German, and Czech. (Yes, Czech. What does that tell you?) Sears catalogs are important documents; seventy microfilm sets of the national catalog have been placed in libraries throughout the state and a reprint of the Sears Texas catalog is in preparation.

Other aspects of Texas material culture have been the subjects of special studies. Willard B. Robinson's *Gone from Texas* (Texas A & M University Press, 1981) is a history of lost architecture, one of those rare books that ties the object to the general patterns of history. Among the most literate and readable books in print on crafts are Georganna Greer's two works on ceramics: *The Meyer Family: Master Potters of Texas* (Trinity University Press, 1971), and *American Stoneware* (Schiffer Publishing, 1981), a more inclusive study that leans heavily on Texas materials. Terry Jordan, a cultural geographer, has written a variety of valuable studies: *German Seed in Texas Soil: Immigrant Farmers in Nineteenth Century Texas* (University of Texas Press, 1966); *Texas Log Buildings: A Folk Architecture* (University of Texas Press, 1978); *Trails to Texas: Southern Roots of Western Cattle Ranching* (University of Nebraska Press, 1981); and, *Texas Graveyards: A Cultural Legacy* (University of Texas Press, 1982). Lonn Taylor and David Warren's *Texas Furniture* (University of Texas Press, 1974); Cecilia Steinfeldt's and Don Stover's *Early Texas Furniture and Decorative Arts* (Trinity University Press, 1973); and Cecilia Steinfeldt's *Texas Folk Art* (Texas Monthly Press, 1981), are valuable sources on artifacts.

These special studies need to be read for comparative purposes against more general studies of artifacts in American life. The books published by the American Association for State and Local History, 708 Berry Road, Nashville, Tennessee 37204, are absolutely indispensible for understanding subjects in local history and for learning how to present them to your audience. A short list of AASLH titles suggests their range: William Seale's *The Tasteful Interlude: American Interiors Through the Camera's Eye, 1860–1917*, and *Recreating the Historic House Interior*; Thomas J. Schlereth's *Artifacts and the American Past* and *Material Culture Studies in America*; David E. Kying and Myron A. Marty's *Nearby History: Exploring the Past Around You*; Fay D. Metcalf and Matthew Downey's *Using Local History in the Classroom*; H. G. Jones' *Local Government Records: An Introduction to Their Management, Preservation, and Use*; and Robert A. Weinstein and Larry Booth's *Collection, Use, and Care of Historical Photographs*. As you become seriously involved in researching and creating history, you'll become familiar with these publications.

These general sources offer a rich and varied understanding of Texas, of artifacts, and of local history. Other types of sources help you focus on specific topics. Originally created to serve purposes entirely different from the uses a historian can make of them, they provide the details that bring the history of a community to life. We will highlight the possibilities that they open for interpreting your community's past.

Newspapers

One of the best written sources is that ongoing chronicle of community history, the local newspaper. Because newspapers trace the flow of events and isolate the subjects that have engaged a community's interest, their pages reveal the flavor of local life. News and feature stories relate community concerns and tell who stood high on the social ladder, what recreations were favored in a town, what crimes and crises took place. Editorials and letters to the editor are a rough index of public opinion; they highlight conflicts. Advertisements and announcements give insight into local taste and cultural life. Obituaries are frequently a source of detailed biographies.

In working with newspapers, especially for the Nineteenth Century, keep two facts in mind. First, the local newspaper often had a news monopoly; no competing electronic media existed to preempt big stories. So, the local paper often focused on national and state news. Nevertheless, much can be gleaned from its pages about local events. Especially where there was constant rivalry between towns, as in the cases of Galveston and Houston or Dallas and Fort Worth, papers from neighboring towns often provide better insight into local events than the local paper. Second, news was transmitted less instantaneously than it is today. Stories often took days or weeks to develop. But they were reported in a florid and colorful language that is often a delight to read and can be a source of good label copy. So be patient and follow a story as it develops.

Public Records

Public records provide details that are otherwise unattainable. At the local government level, probate, civil and criminal court records, land office and tax lists, and vital statistics are generally available. In Texas, public records are now being put on microfilm and housed in regional depositories throughout the state. *Probate records*—wills, inventories, administrator's accounts—will tell you what people thought important enough to pass on to the next generation. All the way back to the Seventeenth Century, Americans have gone to court to solve grievances. *Court records* are extremely important for a close look at our litigious culture. Civil court records provide wonderful descriptions of controversies large and small. Bankruptcy records contain property inventories that provide information on the things that people owned and valued. Criminal court records are a mine of data on patterns of behavior. Other types of records—church papers, fraternal and social organization files, school records—also contain a wealth of detail on day-to-day life.

The federal manuscript censuses are now open through 1910; they list all the questions asked by census takers as they went from house to house through neighborhoods. They reveal ways of life, patterns of wealth, family structure. They can help you place people in their community. Social historians rely heavily on the manuscript census to develop statistical models for understanding local communities. Monographs by social historians will give you frameworks for systematic study of your own community.

City Directories and
Commercial Histories

City directories are another source of detailed, demographic information. They include a fairly full account of the commercial classes in a community, but they omit others. In 1866, the Houston City Directory had only two references to "colored persons" in the city; but the 1870 census lists thousands. (Later, city directories became more inclusive, but you need to be aware of this bias.) City directories also can tell you about community life. They include advertisements that suggest local style, taste, and customs, as well as what goods and services were available. They list the types of jobs people had and the types of businesses that operated in the community. They can be used as a source of good graphic materials; they contain drawings of business establishments, clothing, consumer goods that you can photograph and use in an exhibit.

Many communities also have books of local history which, like city directories, were basically commercial ventures. In the late Nineteenth Century, publishers prepared county histories on speculation by selling advance subscriptions. For additional fees, subscribers could submit their own biographies and have their photographs included in the final product. Even though these narratives were accepted as submitted, commercial histories are worth examining for self-portraits of the local elite, their tastes and attitudes.

Unwritten Sources

Literary sources are only one of the ways to search out facts and to establish contexts. Local historians also read the traces left in unwritten sources. New interpretations come about when we ask new questions about the past and sift through new evidence in search of the answers. One innovative attempt to ask new questions involves an event that has been of interest to historians since it occurred, that has been written about from almost every conceivable interpretive perspective, and that still eludes definitive explanation: the Salem Witch Trials.

In the early 1970's, Paul Boyer and Stephen Nissenbaum, a pair of young historians at Harvard, began to reinvestigate the events leading up to the Salem Witch Trials. They reviewed all the existing interpretations and were unsatisfied with the explanations that had been offered. Then they went back to original written sources—the manuscripts of the city of Salem, court records, contemporary accounts, descriptions of the people involved—and still they got nowhere. The written record had nothing new to say on the problem. So they tried a new approach.

They took a map of Salem, plotted where all the people involved in the controversy lived, and a simple fact became dramatically clear. All the people on one side of the case lived on one side of town; all the people on the other side lived on the other side of town. They began to probe further. Who were these people, how did they earn a living? They identified one group largely as farmers, the other group made their living largely from the sea. And so, they concluded that the trials came about because of a local, economic dispute. By reading the unwritten record, they were able to bring a whole new interpretive approach to an old subject, an interpretation that remains controversial but that has shed new light on a "settled" question.

Maps

Boyer and Nissenbaum listened to what an English historian termed "the testimony of our fields and walls and hedges." The landscape itself is a source that can be read directly and understood through those interpretive aids we call maps. A community's environment—its soils, climate, flora, fauna, topography, natural resources—affected historical choices. The environment determined original options; it shaped subsequent activities; and, it was changed by human action. The arrangement of a community's streets and neighborhoods, farms and commercial districts, highways and transportation routes shows the hand of man on the land. Both the natural and the man-made environment should be experienced first-hand, on foot, by car, or by airplane, to develop a genuine sense of place, and only then explored through maps.

A comparison of maps can deepen your sense of place by showing you how the landscape has changed over time. Maps confirm impressions gathered in the field and offer supporting testimony to your first-hand observations. There are a wide variety of maps that can teach you Texas local history. Among the earliest are land survey maps, or plats. Filed at the county assessor's office, they show first impact—how the land was originally divided and settled. They also offer clues to old roads and sites where buildings or burial grounds stood. Commercial and promotional maps supplement information found in survey maps. "Bird's eye" views, those city maps that were popular from the 1840's into the 1920's, are among the most interesting. Itinerant mapmakers visited a town, sketched its street layout, topography, and buildings, and then extrapolated a panoramic view that showed how the community appeared from a few thousand feet in the air. The publishers promoted their project through the local newspaper and sold subscriptions in advance. Often prominent landmarks were given special treatment in the border of the map.

Over fifty "bird's eye" views of Texas cities were published. It is a fair assumption that their contents are accurate because the mapmakers sold their work to local customers who wanted their homes and businesses correctly represented. The publishers also promoted the community; in some cases, they catered to local pride by showing areas planned for development, but not yet built. These maps should be cross-checked against city directories and other written sources for absolute accuracy. They do offer interesting depictions of the landscape. In some cases, more than one version exists for a single community; and so, they can also show graphically how the town grew. Over 1,100 bird's eye views are housed in the Library of Congress whose photoduplication service department can help you obtain copies for exhibit use.

Itinerant cartographers also produced county maps and atlases for sale to local residents. Subscriptions again were offered and, for additional cost, land owners could have sketches of their homes or businesses included. Based on existing plats and records, they show property owners and property lines, roads and natural features. Other maps were created to generate business: to promote railroad routes, to develop suburbs; to encourage automobile travel; to advertise recreational areas; and to serve a whole range of commercial purposes. They provide a wealth of collateral data. They contain information about how people perceived Texas and how its landscape has changed; and, for some communities, they go back into the late 1860's. They also recreate the flavor of the times. For instance, early automobile touring guides portray the rigors of travel before highways by giving detailed directions for cross-country navigation.

Sanborn maps are a special source of accurate information on the built environment. Beginning in 1877, the Sanborn Map Company produced block by block, building by building, large scale maps of cities in Texas every five to seven years for insurance agents. They include all the information a prudent underwriter would need to write a policy: the strength of the local fire and police departments, the nature of the water system, and the structure, composition, and use of buildings. They tell how buildings were constructed, how fireproof they were, how many floors they had, where fire escapes were located, and what was going on in each structure. They are also accurate dimensional maps, scaled from fifty to four hundred ground feet per map inch, and they are color coded. The Barker Texas History Center at the University of Texas has a complete set for the state up to the early Twentieth Century and copies can still be ordered directly from the Sanborn Map Company, 629 Fifth Avenue, Pelham, New York 10803.

The U.S. Geological Survey has systematically mapped the United States in large scale topographic maps that show both natural features—relief, orchards, woodlands, marshes, water courses—and manmade features like bridges, dams, roads, and structures. The largest scale maps, designated 7½ minute maps, portray two thousand feet on the ground per inch and include abandoned sites—pioneer cemeteries, quarries, building sites. The Texas index map can be obtained from the Information and Data Services, U.S. Geological Survey, 508 National Center, Reston, Virginia, 22092, and will show what is available for your community. Maps will provide an overview of how your community spread out over time, depict original settlement patterns, describe city neighborhoods, and, above all, catch the interest of exhibit viewers.

Particular features of the landscape, the buildings where people live, work, worship, play, all have a story to tell. Both their architecture and their internal arrangement reveal things said and done. We read them by combining visual and written sources with first-hand observation. Recent interest in preserving historic buildings has generated a variety of readily available published material on architectural history, both for Texas and for the nation as a whole. Nominations for historical markers in your community and for the National Register of Historic Places, programs administered through the Texas Historical Commission, include detailed place histories. Architecture and interior decoration have special languages that you can translate into facts of local history.

Visual Materials

For early Texas history, certainly up through the Civil War, paintings, drawings, magazine illustrations, and prints are the primary visual record of things said and done. They confirm literary testimony with a wealth of detail that words alone cannot provide. They exist in relative abundance at many museums, archives, and libraries throughout the state. And they are wonderful interpretive material in exhibits where one picture is worth yards and yards of verbiage.

You can get an idea of original landscapes in Texas through the sketches and paintings of artists who accompanied early expeditions to the state. These pictures give us eyewitness views of terrain merely described in the journals and reports of the explorers. From time to time, the same scenes were sketched by other artists and so offer perspectives on how the landscape changed over time.

Artists also show you the people of Texas, as they actually were or were perceived by others. As early as the 1850's, for instance, through accounts in the national press, Texans were being portrayed as crude, rambunctious, tough Westerners, creating a stereotype that persists today. Publications perpetuated this image through cartoons and drawings and reinforced a popular notion that may or may not have been true, but that has certainly shaped our self-image. Our understanding of the Indian cultures that faded quickly in response to the pressures of Anglo settlement would be foreshortened if written documents were the only source of information. Happily, they are not; and so we have visual depictions of native American life to supplement contemporary written accounts of Indian "depredations."

Photographs

Following the Civil War, another form of visual documentation, photography, was used in Texas to document how communities grew, people lived, and society changed. Like paintings and drawings, photographs seize time and hold a moment for close scrutiny. Because a camera seems to work like the human eye, photographs compel our attention. Because they seem truer-to-life than other visual images, photographs are capable of creating an emotional engagement similar to that aroused by real events. Because they seem to freeze the moment, they convey detailed information about an event and an environment.

So deeply have photography and its sister media, television and film, affected our culture, that we are said to be living in a visual age. Compare the number of people you know that keep a diary to the number that take snapshots and keep photo albums. Since the late Nineteenth Century, history has been recorded largely through photographic imagery. For local history, photographs are perhaps the most abundant single source of visual information. To deal with this primary record of our times, you should learn to read as well as to look at photographs. Systematically approached, photographs can be a rich source of authentic information.

Although they seem to capture reality, photographs do not do so at random. They are the contrived, conscious creations of different photographers and so you must first consider the maker's intent. Why was a particular photograph taken? From what viewpoint? For what purpose? Even though the image stands alone and seems to speak for itself, questions about its origin help you frame an understanding of its content. Begin, then, with the maker and develop a sense of what he or she was trying to say through the photograph. The result is always the product of man and man-made mechanism; behind the shutter is the eye of the photographer who must choose the moment to trip the shutter.

That moment has itself three characteristics: it is framed, composed, and detailed. The frame is simply the border around the picture; it encloses a content, and it excludes other information that would have been available to an actual participant and would have produced a different view. The frame contains the setting of the photograph, its time and place; and, the frame determines the internal arrangement of a photograph's parts, its composition. Each photograph is composed of a series of smaller pictures which blend to create a total image. What a photograph has to say is contained in these small details and in the patterns that make up their relationships.

Is the photograph posed or spontaneous? Is it a close-up or a middle distance shot? Is it simple or complex in its content? What does the photograph suggest about the quality of the scene it depicts: serentiy or activity; drama or repose; chaos or order? What sounds, colors, smells are implied by its subject matter?

Relationships between people are suggested by simple things, physical space between them or whether they are touching one another. Faces reveal moods and emotions. A family portrait clearly has a different feeling than a group shot made at a company picnic, a feeling that can be read in the expressions and in body language of people.

The objects in a photograph reveal social class, self perceptions, tastes, occupations, concerns. Pay close attention to the cut and condition of clothing, the style of household decorations and their abundance, possessions intentionally displayed or accidentally included, architecture, and the natural landscape. Put yourself imaginatively into the scene. You may have been put into situations similar to those captured on film. Your imagination—your personal sense of how it might have been—is a valid guide to what a picture means.

The photographic record of Texas is rich and extensive. The best sources of local photographs are out there in your communities: in private collections, in school and church archives, and in the trunks and boxes in your neighbor's attic. Collect first at home, and then explore the resources housed elsewhere. From the last half of the Nineteenth Century to the present, the photo-history of Texas grows like yeast, geometrically, decade by decade.

In the 1890's for instance, a photographer named Henry Stark began the first intentional and systematical survey of life in the state. His collection is now housed at the Dallas Historical Society and it reveals that behind the rural exterior of Texas lay the beginnings for an industrial and commercial state. Other photographers have followed his impulse ever since. Those who worked for the Farm Security Administration captured many aspects of Texas life during the 1930's. Each FSA photographer was an especially careful, talented observer. Their work is so thoroughly documented that it might still be possible to interview people portrayed. FSA photographers visited many, many towns in the state; their collection is now at the Library of Congress.

During the 1940's, the Standard Oil Company set out to document oil production through a project organized by Roy Stryker, the man who had directed the Farm Security Administration photographers. Thousands of Texas photographs, emphasizing communities involved in the oil industry, are now housed in the Standard Oil Collection at the University of Louisville. Local newspaper files also contain a great variety of historical and contemporary photographs that continue the visual record of ordinary life and its extraordinary events.

Visual materials can be used both to unlock the past and to help you interpret it. Their dual role as research sources and as exhibit material underscores a theme that should be familiar to you by now. Not only do different sources speak to you, they also speak to each other, they corroborate the testimony that each gives separately. Listen to the singers and to the song. Conceive your search broadly and cover all sorts of sources. The moral of the story is clear: if you hope to reach a wide audience, you have to cast a wide net and use a variety of materials to understand things said and done and to communicate your understanding.

3

THINGS
LEFT BEHIND

A portion of the material presented in Chapter Three was developed for the workshops by Conover Hunt, formerly Chief Curator at the Dallas Historical Society and now an independent consultant.

Chapter 3:

THINGS LEFT BEHIND

ARTIFACTS ARE ACTUAL PIECES OF THE PAST, three-dimensional and palpable survivors from points in time that are no more. A woman's side-saddle, a soldier's britches, an apple peeler, a stock certificate, an oil lamp, a cashbox, a clock-winding key, a window frame, a doll with a wax face—all these are objects that you can see and experience for yourself, things that you can hold in your hands just as they were grasped by the people who originally held them. Objects require you to depend upon your own senses: to feel, first-hand, the heft of a hammer, without knowing its weight on a scale.

Because artifacts may be seen directly, touched and handled, lifted, moved, smelled, worn, thumped, plucked, played, or used, artifacts are real and present in a way that other historical sources are not. But to *satisfy* the curiosity of your hand and the appetite of your eye and mind, you will have to treat artifacts like other historical sources; you will have to understand and interpret them.

Artifacts embody the ideas, values, beliefs, and interests of their makers and users; artifacts reflect the culture that produced them. Artifacts inspire emotional responses. But artifacts will not do these things of and by themselves; as a historian, you will look to artifacts for the meaning implicit in the relationships among each object, its cultural context, and your own time and place. You will have to make these mute things speak.

Your challenge is to make explicit what artifacts are and represent, to treat artifacts like other historical facts and to make them convey their meanings. As you read them carefully, artifacts give up useful evidence about themselves, about the society they came from, and about the relationship of that society to your own.

Information that you recover through physical contact helps you begin to understand what an object is and means. Physical properties—weight, shape, texture, design—that give an artifact dimension and form also tell you about its function. They help you understand its *identity*.

Artifacts also have a particular capacity to suggest the circumstances that produced them, their *context*. Physical remnants are often the only surviving evidence of people who have left no other record. Our understanding of prehistoric and preliterate cultures is based principally on the things those cultures left behind. But what of the lives of Nineteenth Century Texas farm families, people not given to writing autobiographies or memoirs? Artifacts also reveal the history of non-literate people, of anonymous men and women who were counted in the census or described by literate contemporaries, but who themselves left no written record. Artifacts represent a broader cross-section of the population than may be accessible through other sources. Because common objects were the materials of daily life, they can recall tastes, customs, manners, domestic routines, working conditions, values, and attitudes. Artifacts carry primary data about basic living conditions: how chores were performed, meals served, children raised, and daily life was led. Artifacts can show us the preoccupations of ordinary people.

Third, artifacts may evoke an emotional response. For the people who used them as well as for us, they come to represent more than what they are or what they say about their original context. Because objects are valued by people, they may call up a variety of feelings, ideas, or memories. These mental connections exist in our relationship to an object; they are its *associations*. Associations may be unrelated to an artifact's physical character or to what it suggests about its environment, but they are also part of an artifact's meaning.

Reading Artifacts

Identity, context, and associations are the categories of information contained in artifacts. To read objects, you have to systematically decode three messages: first, an artifact's physical character; second, its social reality; and, third, its associations. In this process, you move from the artifact itself to its historical environment and finally to its significance. At each state, you attempt to retrieve in words the data that is concretely embodied in objects and in men's preceptions of them.

To read successfully an artifact, you first describe and evaluate it by making judgments about its authenticity, design, and the other qualities that make up its identity. To recover its context, you analyze the relationship between an artifact and the culture that produced it. To understand its significance, you interpret associations in order to state the relationship between an artifact and human experience.

When you go from the artifact itself to its context and associations, you are following the same steps that others who later confront the same object will be taking to satisfy their curiosity. In a survey, visitors to Colonial Williamsburg reported that 70 percent of their initial reactions to objects on exhibit involved questions about identity. Visitors first try to name an unfamiliar artifact, often by giving it a modern term. They plug it into their personal data bank and then check the correctness of their initial response by reading an exhibit label. After they have named it, they begin to deepen their sense of its identity by evaluating whether the object is real, asking how it worked or when it was used. Visitors move from identifying and describing an artifact into questions of context and associations.

When you examine an artifact, first ask yourself about the artifact's physical properties:

What is it made of?
What are its dimensions?

Shape?
Weight?
Texture?
Colors?

Since you use objects in your daily life and you live in an environment filled with artifacts, you will have an intuitive feel for the answers to these questions and you can, with confidence, bring your personal experience into play—*but* you must do background research and *cross-check* your intuition against other sources.

Most artifacts are designed to do something; so, describing an object takes you to the next questions:

How does it work?
When was it made?
By whom? How?
What was this object for?
How was it used?

Some artifacts extend your senses and your power over the environment. Optical instruments allow you to see farther and deeper. Communication devices multiply the range of your voice and ear. Tools expand your reach and physical capabilities. Other artifacts express inner needs. Flags symbolize group identity, patriotism, duty, scriptures, beliefs and spiritual longings. Paintings embody delight in color and harmony; sculpture, sense of form and proportion. Frequently, an object contains both practical and symbolic meanings. For instance, cowboy clothing is functionally designed to protect its wearer, but it also represents workmanship and design, symbolizes courage and aggressiveness, and embodies a social order and level of technological development.

While you are describing an artifact and its uses, you are also evaluating it. After you accumulate information on its physical qualities, material, design, history, construction, and use, you should also decide whether an object is authentic, well designed, rare, valuable, important. Evaluation involves judgments about quality of workmanship, expressiveness of form, and similar aesthetic elements.

After you grasp the physical reality of an artifact, you are ready to explore its social meaning, its *context*. Your goal at this state is, in Heny Glassie's phrase, to get at the people behind an artifact. Having acquired a good sense of the object itself, you can begin to draw out its connections to the culture that produced it. An artifact's role leads to questions about an artifact's immediate environment:

> Who used it?
> In what circumstance?
> How often?
> In conjunction with what other objects?
> Where did it come from?
> Where has it been?

Many artifacts also carry symbolic information about their original environment. Guns, for instance, suggest the roles that American men have traditionally played as soldiers, hunters, and heads of families. The design of house interiors reveals values placed on privacy and on family group activities. The Statue of Liberty is a monument and a symbol of America's values, of its self-image, and of its role in the world.

Because all artifacts exist within a chronology, they represent stages in the solution of problems. A society's technological capabilities, the limits that its physical environment set on human behavior, even the dominant traits of a given time, can be understood by the things created to solve practical problems and to serve symbolic functions. By comparing similar artifacts over time, you will get a sense of historical change. By comparing similar objects used in the same period, you also will develop a cross-cultural perspective, a sense of the differences between cultures. Claw hammers came into use with the availability of wire nails; lighter hammers were developed when steel processing improved and when the use of balloon frame house construction spread in the United States. American axes differed early in their design from European models, just as American automobiles still do. Sad irons and steam irons are part of a network that involves a specific source of heat, types of fabric, styles of clothing, and even conventions of dress.

Practical, symbolic, and comparative analysis allow you to

figure out the original context of an artifact. When you consider its associations, you turn from the people behind the artifact to yourself. Having established what the artifact is and meant in a broad sense historically, you now complete your reading by saying what it can tell you about your culture. Here, you are finding out and saying why it is important to understand this particular object.

Associations are the wide variety of subsequent meanings that artifacts carry into the present. Some artifacts communicate culturally universal associations. A Kiowa cradle board, for instance, will suggest motherhood wherever it is viewed. Other associations are based on similarities between your audience's history and the experiences of the people who originally owned and used an object. A Model T Ford, in this case, would evoke similar meanings for Americans whose particular experiences differ. The affective, emotional messages contained in cradle boards, Model T Fords, and other objects, are important parts of what artifacts have to say.

Using Artifacts

In rural communities in the United States as late as 1880, one child in five did not reach the age of six. This fact can be recovered from different sources: census figures, newspaper obituaries, letters, even from tombstones in the local cemetery—and can be communicated in words. But when it is embodied in an exhibit with a child's small, white coffin and a series of postmortem photographs, this statistical reality takes on a concrete and personal meaning. The message of a real coffin and a handful of faded photographs reveals the power of what Barbara Tuchman has called "history by the ounce," the use of concrete details to convey an experience more vividly than words alone.

Artifacts like these force an audience to respond emotionally, to feel their message before digesting it intellectually. Artifacts bring an audience into conversation with an exhibit by working through their responses and by allowing them to connect their own impressions with the story they are being told.

Be aware of the power of real things. The right artifacts can say what you mean in the fullest possible sense. They can provide those details that remain in the visitor's memory when the words used to describe them are long forgotten. Some objects are so powerful that they transcend the barriers of time and place. They speak to ageless, universal aspects of the human condition. They contain the meanings and associations that were there originally. And in the new context of an exhibit, they build a series of impressions that create new meanings. A child's coffin conveys both the grief and loss that his family experienced a hundred years ago, and the harsh, tenuous quality of life that our great-grandparents faced almost daily.

You need to be conscious of the pitfalls in using objects. A common temptation is overloading your interpretation with too many artifacts. When you put objects together, their relationships create new meanings. When you group sets of artifacts sequentially, you are building a series of impressions. When many artifacts deliver slightly different messages, you risk putting your visitor into a situation similar to being in a crowded room where the conversations of people blend into a general din and cannot be distinguished. Resist the tendency to overcrowd; select the fewest number of objects that say best what you mean. When you use more than one artifact, be sure that the meanings reinforce one another when possible. Try also to use artifacts that are in good condition. Yes, historical artifacts are worn, soiled, and rarely in perfect condition. But a spring protruding from a broken chair still says "Fix me," and louder than anything else you wish to communicate.

Second, conscientiously avoid the "moonlight-and-magnolia" syndrome, the tendency to romanticize the past and ignore its less desirable features. In recreating room settings to portray a period, you can fall into the trap of oversimplifying the complexity of real life. Historic houses did not have furniture in pristine condition, nor were all their furnishings from the same period. Rooms were not always elegant and tasteful in their decoration. Every object should be substantiated by research into its origin and into the probability that it really belongs in the context being represented. Be aware of present-mindedness, the unconscious tendency to read our contemporary tastes, values, and attitudes into the past. Recall the hair-dos favored by actresses in early Hollywood westerns; marcelled waves popular during the 1930's appeared on most of the heroines behaving heroically in the movies' version of the 1880's.

Third, steer a safe course between overgeneralizing from a single artifact and saying too little about it. Overgeneralizing makes a categorical statement from an unrepresentative sample. Was this wedding gown typical of bridal fashion in 1890? Or is it representative of only a small, fairly well-to-do sample of the population? Saying too little about an artifact results in a series of short identification labels, like "sad iron, circa 1880." Why was it called a "sad" iron? How did it work? What does it say about domestic life? Adding a phrase about an artifact's significance or origin helps the audience make connections between your story and the objects that tell it.

Fourth, to select the best artifacts, have a concept in mind before you begin to collect material. Know the story that you want to tell and how you plan to present it. Part of your responsibility in marking the Sesquicentennial is to bring a sense of roots to people new to Texas by teaching them where the community came from and showing them how they fit in. At the heart of community life and of community history is the complex web of connections that every person forms with other men and women to do the things that we cannot do alone: earn a living, raise a family, worship and play, die and be born.

Seek out artifacts that reflect broadly the lives of the many rather than the few. Because personal clothing is both sculptural and biographical, it creates a sense of the reality of the past and its people. But while virtually everyone wore every-day clothing, they wore it everyday and they wore it out. Little daily apparel has survived. So, do fancy wedding gowns, for-mal wear, and military uniforms convey a true picture of daily life for the majority of your community?

Furniture, dishes, and decorative articles carry personal connotations and reveal tastes, influences on the community, and lifestyles. When you use these artifacts, be particularly sensitive to the ones that have modern counterparts. They are keys that your audience will grasp immediately. In your selec-tion, try again to reflect the diversity of the community. Re-member that everyone did not eat dinner from expensive, handpainted French china, even though these heirlooms have been preserved. Be conscious of the people who did not make it into the history books and did not use fine objects. Find out how they lived and what they used; include that information in the overall story.

Fifth, consider using graphic materials as objects in an ex-hibit. Select a line or two, a special phrase excerpted from a document, have it photographically enlarged, and display the result rather than the document itself. Not many visitors will stop to read an entire document. Advertisements, playbills, and books reveal tastes and influences from outside the local community that had an impact on it. They add color and per-sonality to an exhibit, especially when they echo other, tan-gible things—clothing, housewares, tools—that you have on exhibit.

The best part of using artifacts is the treasure hunt itself. Where will you find things left behind? Where memories are kept, out there in trunks, attics, barns, and in the hearts of people in your community. A Texas Sesquicentennial project will give you the opportunity to collect bits of history and, in the process, to build the sort of support and enthusiasm that will make the project a success. Seek out other community historians: antique dealers, collectors, museum curators, and ask them to help you read objects.

❧·❀·❧
Artifactual Ideas

The distinguishing characteristic of historical exhibits is that they present interpretations grounded in and based upon real things. Exhibits are designed around "artifactual ideas," concepts that can best be transmitted through perceptions about objects. When you begin your search for artifacts, have a story in mind, an interpretation that you wish to present. To select the artifacts that will tell that story, you must also understand the medium that you will be using.

A historical exhibit is neither a book on a wall nor a series of images; it is a selective combination of artifacts with words and images, placed within a special environment to create history. Exhibits are ill-equipped to deal with abstractions which are best presented in words alone. Yes, all exhibits begin with abstractions, but they create meanings primarily through the actual objects they contain. Words and graphic images support this endeavor. Their role is to lead visitors to the messages you wish to present.

An exhibit's final form is the result of interaction between the story you wish told and the objects that will show it. To create an exhibit, you continually refine abstract ideas into concrete representations of the world they describe. Like all creative processes, this refinement requires an act of faith on your part. To speak through artifacts, you must assume that the audience's perceptions will lead it to your meaning. You shape your message through your audience's experience of real things. You rely on the power of artifacts to create impressions that will carry your story.

4

CREATING
HISTORY
BY DESIGN

A portion of the material presented in Chapter Four was developed for the workshops by Sam Hoyle, Director of the U.S. Army Air Defense Artillery Museum, Fort Bliss and David Ross, Director of the McAllen International Museum.

Chapter 4:

CREATING HISTORY BY DESIGN

AFTER YOU HAVE INVESTIGATED THE EVIDENCE which contains the facts of history, and after you have interpreted those facts to find their pattern and meaning, then you are ready to make the facts and your interpretations live for an audience. There's a special means of communication through which you can engage people directly: the historical exhibit. Exhibits selectively bring the facts of history—words, images, objects—together in a new environment. Historical exhibits combine the goal of written and visual history, a meaningful story, with the tangible reality of historical materials on display. For those who visit them, exhibits create a memory of things said and done both through what is exhibited and through how the exhibit is arranged.

To design and produce an effective historical exhibit, you will need:

1. A sense of your *audience*;
2. A carefully limited and clearly defined *concept* that you wish to convey; and,
3. An understanding of *design*, how you can bring that concept to your audience.

Audience

Exhibits can reach audiences who lack the time or interest in other forms of history. People who do not read books or attend visual programs will tour an exhibit. Serious and informed scholars will tour an exhibit. Some visitors come to an exhibit for entertainment and diversion. Some come to learn. Most expect to be touched by what they see and to discuss the exhibit with each other—on the spot or after they have left. Confronted with real pieces of the past, actively and emotionally engaged by them, visitors are thus predisposed to accept an exhibit's interpretation as true. Historical exhibits speak authoritatively to a large group of people who partake of both the medium and the message.

The audience's relationship with an exhibit shapes what you can say through it. Visitors participate on their own terms and at their own pace. They move freely and often at random through its space, exploring what it contains. Typically, viewers spend less than a minute in front of any one display. While the amount of information you can provide is limited by this pattern of behavior, visitor expectations allow you to speak with impact *through moments created to engage their attention.* Your task is to design an exhibit with the knowledge of this pattern of selective attention, shared interaction, and sporadic engagement.

Concept

Behind every exhibit is an idea that you wish to present. Historical exhibits convey understandings of the past through a series of objects arranged in an ordered sequence and supported by labels and graphic aids. Your research will suggest themes that might be developed through an exhibit. The possibilities are virtually limitless. They range from broad topics, like the overall history of your community, to the narrower themes that make up its story.

Begin to translate your ideas into an exhibit by drafting an outline of the story you wish to tell. Each section of the outline should start with a clear and emphatic statement of purpose. In a sentence or two, limit and define your objective. Your statement of purpose serves the same role that a thesis sentence does for a book: statements of purpose force you to begin to narrow the scope of your exhibit, to express a point of view about your topic, and to consider how you may best present it. If, for instance, you wish to deal with the sweep of your community's history, you might express your purpose this way: "to trace the pattern of community growth and highlight the factors that caused it."

You already have a series of assertions that need to be substantiated: that there has indeed been growth, and that its causes and consequences can be isolated and described. You have also created a series of questions that need to be addressed: What do you mean by growth and how can it be described? What factors propelled growth and how can those factors be represented? As you search for answers, you will begin to see whether your idea, as it is currently conceived, will, in fact, develop into an exhibit.

Once you have answered these questions and others, you can divide your topic into units that may become the bases for a series of related displays. Select the major divisions of your topic by following the logic implied in your statements of purpose. In our example, this means first that you determine what constitutes your community—exactly *which* place are you going to present—and select periods of time to show its growth. Within these limits, you next have to consider what sort of pattern unfolded and how. Decide what factors were responsible for this sequence and consider how these may be embodied in your exhibit. Working through these steps will suggest ways of ordering your subject and will help you further define its scope.

The difficulty of subdividing and ordering a set of ideas may be met successfully with a standard research tool: the *index card*. As topics suggest themselves, summarize them on separate cards. Place a short headline phrase at the top of the card and use an abbreviation to indicate how the idea will be represented in an exhibit. Four symbols cover the range of possible materials: A, an artifact; G, a graphic, e.g., map, diagram, art work; P, photograph; and T, text. The total number of cards will indicate the space ideally suited to your concept. Comparing this ideal space to the actual space available will help you refine the topic. Sorting the cards will also suggest satisfactory relationships, sequences, and subtopics that you may want to drop or expand.

After you have completed a working outline, draft an *exhibit script*. In writing your exhibit script, you begin to realize your ideas. Your script follows the major subdivisions of your outline; each section begins with a summary. In two or three short paragraphs, you detail the purpose of each particular section, its place in the story line, and its objectives. Below your summary, list the concepts that are to be expressed and the objects and interpretive aids in that will embody them.

Divide your exhibit script into four vertical columns. In the first column, state the particular idea or ideas that will be represented through objects and interpretive materials. Then list side by side in the second and third columns, objects and materials, respectively. Interpretive materials include images and words, the illustrations and the text that tie an object and concept together. The fourth column specifies the type of display—case, panel, free-standing or suspended—that might best present the materials.

Translating your interpretation into a preliminary exhibit script is the critical first stage in planning any exhibit. It forces you to decide which artifacts, words, and images can be used to evoke the proper visitor responses and carry your meaning. The result of your efforts is a detailed exhibit concept, a meaningful story complete with a description of the artifacts, images, words, and fixtures that will express it.

Design

Design is the process of converting a concept into tangible reality. Simply put, any design is a solution to a particular problem. Every form of communication—publications, films, audio-visual programs, and exhibits—poses certain questions that must be addressed to fit message to medium and to *communicate* with your audience. For full explanations of considerations only briefly described here, you'll want to read four basic and indispensible books. All four are available from the American Association for State and Local History, 708 Berry Road, Nashville, Tennessee 37204.

Arminta Neal, formerly curator of exhibits for the Denver Museum of Natural History, has written two handbooks on the specifics of planning, design, construction, and installation: *Exhibits for the Small Museum: A Handbook* (1976) and *Help! For the Small Museum: Handbook of Exhibit Ideas and Methods* (1969). Both books offer practical advice on details such as scripts, layouts, case construction, space requirements, wiring, and lighting. Both are illustrated with drawings, diagrams, and photographs. The 1976 volume expands on material in the first work and includes references to it, so both should be read together. Lothar P. Witteborg's *Good Show! A Practical Guide for Temporary Exhibits* (1981) focuses on the installation of traveling exhibits and contains information on panel and case construction, scheduling, and other practical matters. Beverly Serrell's *Marking Exhibit Labels: A Step-by-Step Guide* (1983) is exactly that: the best single source on planning, writing, producing, and evaluating the words that describe objects and give them additional meaning.

You should be thoroughly familiar with the ideas in these four essential books before tackling an exhibit project. Their total cost is under $60. By showing you the steps involved in preparing an exhibit, these books allow you to see how feasible your project will be, given the resources—time, budget, personnel, and space—that you can devote to it. These books will guide you step-by-step through the tasks involved into designing and building an exhibit.

Here, we will outline the process of exhibit design by examining the characteristics of exhibits as a means of communication. Your basic goal is to invite the audience to participate, to offer them an enjoyable and aesthetically pleasing experience. The exhibit script begins this process. Planning a design takes the process one step further; it moves your concept towards physical reality. That reality has three parts: (1) an environment; (2) the physical structures placed into it; and (3) the interpretive materials that are contained within them.

An exhibit's environment communicates at a nonverbal level to establish a setting and an overall mood for the exhibit's contents. The space that an exhibit occupies, its layout, displays, lighting, colors, and textures carry this nonverbal message. These elements of design unify the presentation and attract the visitor's attention to the exhibit. Design elements have to be appropriate to the exhibit's theme, subordinate to the interpretive materials the exhibit contains, and evocative of the concept it presents.

Layout and Displays

An exhibit's space is three-dimensional; its height as well as its length and width should be approximated through a floor plan. The purpose of a floor plan is two-fold: (1) to bridge the transition from an exhibit concept to an exhibit plan, and, (2) to create a layout that is in character with the space available and with the visitors' expectations. Because you are designing for people, you need to plan for their physical needs. Build these assumptions about visitors into your plans: most people steer to the right; they come in groups; they read best at eye level; and, their feet get tired.

In making your floor plan, consider the flow and sequence of visitor traffic through the exhibit space. By designing the space to channel visitors through a predetermined sequence of events to a conclusion, you create a linear patten of interaction that is like a walk through an old-fashioned cafeteria line. You may allow your audience a freer, more random engagement by creating an open format which groups displays into thematic areas, each of which develops the concept. Like a smorgasbord spread out on many tables in a large room, an open pattern is a richer visual environment—but it presents a more complex design challenge.

Historical exhibits often combine both linear and open patterns in ways appropriate to the themes being presented. Exhibits usually include alcoves of cases and several free standing floor pieces to add variety to a linear, chronological pattern. An exhibit's overall exposition should anticipate the tendency of most visitors to move toward the right. Its layout also needs to provide adequate viewing space. Larger objects require a greater viewing distance; dramatic displays of any size attract a crowd. People need room to circulate. Wide aisles should be built into any floor plan.

Every other adult American wears glasses; many older people wear bifocals. Lengthy, written material should be clearly legible and placed slightly below an average line of sight. A height of five feet and three inches is used to approximate eye level in most museums. Large print titles can be placed above eye level since they are more visible. When large objects soar above eye level, you should plan for spaces that allow the visitor to back away to take them in.

Because fatigue is an inevitable part of the visitor's experience in exhibits, you should also provide opportunities for your visitors to rest. The simplest resting places are railings, usually thirty inches high, placed in front of displays that permit visitors to lean. Benches, fifteen inches high, should also be considered for parts of the layout. Not only will these benches accommodate the needs of older visitors, they will encourage *all* visitors to take in an exhibit at their leisure.

Drawing the floor plan requires you to make some decisions about the types of displays that will occupy the visitor's attention: panels, cases, and free-standing or suspended units. Taken together, these displays *are* the immediate environment, the foreground of an exhibit. Each has a specific purpose.

Panels carry introductory labels, summary labels, concluding labels, graphics, design motifs, and, sometimes, artifacts. Constructed of plywood, framed with lumber, and covered with paint, fabric, or vinyl, panels may be free-standing or mounted on a wall.

Cases range in size from plexiglass boxes mounted on pedestal bases to wall-hung or floor-mounted display cases. Cases are the principle medium for artifact display.

Free-standing displays are generally large, single objects mounted on a raised base or hung from the ceiling. They add the drama of real-life scale to an exhibit, but they require additional viewing space.

When you begin to sketch displays for an exhibit space, you should supplement the two-dimensions represented by the floor plan with *elevation drawings*: thumbnail sketches of individual displays that indicate their height, contents, and design. Floor plans and elevation drawings bring exhibit planning to the stage when a *scale model* may be constructed.

Built out of light-weight cardboard, reinforced by balsa wood, on a base scaled ¼ inch to 1 foot, a scale model offers a three-dimensional view of proposed exhibit structures and the space they require. A model can be an extremely useful tool throughout the design process because it visualizes the impact of structures in a way no two-dimensional diagram can. Human figures scaled to the model may be placed and moved around in the model to show how the exhibit will appear to an audience. A scale model portrays how visitor traffic will move through the space. It will also show an exhibit's visual flow and reveal sight lines as well as spatial relationships that you can refine in the final design. Consider a model a changeable instrument that will lead you to try out new configurations.

Color and Texture

Color choices involve base and accent tones. The rules are fairly simple in theory; in practice, their application depends upon the period to be dealt with, the mood you wish to convey, the theme of the exhibit, and the interpretive materials in the exhibit. Background colors should complement the exhibit as a whole and direct attention towards what the exhibit contains. Colors may be used to change visitors' perceptions of the size and shape of a space. Dark shades appear to shrink space; light tones enlarge space. (Dark colors can also hide distractions on the ceiling.) Background colors set a tone for an exhibit. Barn red, for instance, is appropriate for an agricultural exhibit; a very pale blue can suggest an arctic climate. Some shades also carry their own independent meanings. A warm tone like red, which is frequently used as a corridor color, suggsts movement—and may actually hurry your visitors through an exhibit space when you would rather have them linger. A few accent colors may be used to focus attention on key elements of the exhibit, such as main label lettering or special display sections. Unity and simplicity are the keys; too many competing shades may shatter the overall mood you wish to convey.

Texture and color within individual displays should complement and suggest the meaning of the objects they serve. Fine items like china or silver imply a gracious setting, and silk or velvet can provide an appropriate background for them. Burlap fits commonplace objects, wood shavings, placed along the floor of a case containing carpentry tools, or straw in a case of farm implements, indicate function. Decorative elements like type faces or graphic designs, unify a presentation and suggest its content. A fairly common practice in historical exhibits is to represent decades or eras through the use of a type face that was popular during the time represented. Art Deco lettering evokes the 1920's; elaborate scrollwork, the 1890's. A recurring motif, a design or figure, may also serve the same purpose.

Lighting

Because the eye is drawn to areas that are illuminated, lighting is the single most dramatic element in exhibit design. Focused light may be used to highlight individual objects, to lead visitors from one display to another, and to dramatize the exhibit. At the entrance to an exhibit, you should provide a transition area where visitors can pause to let their eyes adjust to the light level within the exhibit and prepare themselves to take the exhibit in. Ambient light is overall illumination; the character and intensity of ambient light creates an atmosphere and expresses a mood for an exhibit as a whole. By varying the relation between light and shadow and by using different light sources, you can make an atmosphere that is warm or cool, sharp-edged or soft, and, you will affect the color values within the exhibit. Accent lighting highlights elements within an exhibit by emphasizing the form and surface qualities of three-dimensional objects or by spotlighting a label or photograph.

Ideally, exhibit spaces should be illuminated entirely by artificial light because artifical light can be manipulated—focused, intensified, dimmed, and moved—to the best advantage of an exhibit's environment and contents. Natural light is undependable and dangerous to objects because it transmits ultraviolet radiation which will damage artifacts. Fluorescent light also emits ultraviolet rays, but UV filter sleeves will help solve this problem. Fluorescent light provides even illumination, is available in warm or cold colors, and works best as ambient or general lighting. Incandescent light is available in a variety of fixtures including flood and spot lights and so is the best source of accent light. Incandescent lamps are low in ultraviolet radiation but will give off heat which may damage material closeby. Consider lighting from the *visitor's* as well as the designer's point of view; place your fixtures carefully, and then adjust them once the exhibit is complete. Lighting is critical to the impact of the overall presentation. If you neglect your lighting, your effort to design an environment will be incomplete.

Build flexibility into the process of designing your exhibit—and be prepared to improvise! Colors, textures, and lighting create a setting for the concepts that you wish to present. Now let's turn from the exhibit environment to the reason for it: the artifacts and labels that will convey your ideas.

Artifacts

Exhibits are designed around objects; the purpose of an exhibit is to draw out ideas implicit in the materials on display. Artifacts convey impressions that impart information and evoke responses. The elements of design are tools that you use to create settings congruent with all an artifact has to say and with what you wish to emphasize about it.

Take, for instance, a pair of forceps used to assist difficult births. In the Nineteenth Century, forceps usually were wrapped with gauze to protect the newborn's head. Before the existence of germs was widely accepted, the gauze wrappings were changed infrequently. Result: a high rate of mortality among mothers whose deliveries were assisted with forceps. The very instrument designed to preserve life brought death. In an exhibit, a pair of nineteenth-century obstetrical forceps becomes very evocative—when the display of the forceps suggests their impact. Mounted in a case with a bright red background, wrapped in frayed gauze, suspended in an open position, backed up with a label that does no more than report the statistics of post-natal fatalities, a pair of forceps will speak directly to the visitor. If you can make other objects speak directly, leading the audience to piece details together, never telegraphing your conclusions, artifacts have greater impact than if muffled in overly explicit explanations.

Select the best artifacts to carry your meaning. The best artifacts contain basic, elemental facts for your visitors to take home. Given the short time visitors will devote to any one display, your message must be immediately understandable. Does each display have a point of focus, an area containing an object or small grouping of objects that the display is designed around? Do the display's color and texture reinforce your message by suggesting function, context, and associations? Do lighting and arrangement focus attention? Does the position in which an object is placed help the visitor extract its meaning? An axe poised in mid-arc or a rifle placed in a horizontal firing position will allow visitors to understand function at first glance so that they can begin to explore wider implications. In using artifacts to tell a story, you work with the impressions they create. These reinforce meaning and draw the visitor into interpreting the wider significance of the artifacts.

Words and Pictures

Interpretive materials encourage and enable the process of inquiry and discovery. Words and pictures give voice to artifacts by connecting your exhibit's concept to its contents and to your design. Interpretive materials provide continuity among a series of displays and smooth the visitor's path from display to display. In short, words and pictures serve the exhibit primarily as signs which inform, direct, and explain. Words and pictures do not carry the weight of interpretation; that is the job of your exhibit as a whole. In a book, words and pictures are the sole means of reaching an audience; in an exhibit, words and pictures are supporting players.

The same rule that applies to artifacts governs your use of words and pictures as interpretive details: select the best and the least. Your goal is to arouse your visitors' curiosity and to encourage them to examine artifacts closely. Sometimes a display will say so much visually that words are unnecessary. A strong graphic—a map, a drawing, or a photograph—may convey enough information to suggest an object's significance. When visitors discover meaning on their own and without being nudged verbally, the impact of the display is heightened.

While the best exhibits hold moments of purely non-verbal communication, all exhibits must use words to secure their meaning. Planning labels is, thus, an extremely important step in exhibit design. You should keep three considerations in mind as you prepare each label: the label's purpose, its intended audience, and its structure.

A title label simply names the exhibit; it attracts attention, conveys the theme, and is typically no more than ten words in length. Subhead labels serve the same function at the same length for sections within an exhibit. Together, titles and subheads resemble headlines and headings in a newspaper story. They tie an exhibit together and indicate its structure. They are set in the large type so they can be seen from a distance, and they may be used as a decorative element in exhibit design.

Main labels introduce or conclude the exhibit as a whole and explain each of the sections that comprise it. Main labels may run from fifty to two hundred words in length. They present general concepts and explain the theme or content of the objects that follow. Main labels are set in a medium-sized type, placed at eye level, and written so that the most important information is placed first. They serve the same purpose a lead paragraph does in a newspaper story. They should be structured so that a reader will grasp the point of an exhibit or display quickly and thus be prepared for specific details.

Group labels, captions, and identification statements interpret individual objects. Group labels may range from fifty to one hundred words; they explain a number of related artifacts by providing information that bridges the gap between the main labels and captions or identification statements. They may be used to develop a theme common to the artifacts on display or to relate the main label to them.

Captions are brief concrete statements about individual objects. They point out details to look for, relate objects to the general themes of the exhibit, and provide information that deepens a visitor's understanding.

Identification labels simply list data about an object: its technical name, date, origin, material, and, perhaps, the donor. (Identification labels are typically the only labels used in art exhibits.)

Designed to present different levels of information, your labels taken together serve the range of interests that visitors bring to an exhibit. Because title and subhead labels orient visitors, they will generally be read by all. Visitors also read some main labels, especially those that introduce and conclude an exhibit. All visitors sample main labels within the exhibit; only a few will read them in their entirety. Group labels, captions, and identification labels are also sampled.

Remember that visitors do not come to an exhibit intent on reading labels. No matter how carefully you prepare labels, not all of them will be read. You should not try to make an exhibit a well-arranged collection of words illustrated by objects. By trying to say too much through words, you may discourage visitors and prevent them from interpreting an exhibit on their own. When you plan labels, keep your visitors in mind. Most adults read 250–300 words a minute; but they will typically spend less than a minute in front of a display. Visitors are curious and they want to be informed. Sometimes they will linger, but they also are distracted by detail. A long, complicated label will discourage them; they are standing on their feet, they may be with a friend or family members, and they may have difficulty concentrating on what the label has to say.

If you want your words to arouse visitors' curiosity and to encourage them to explore, ask yourself: What will visitors want to know and what can be said to grab their attention?

What visitors want to know depends upon the purpose each label serves. Titles and subheads give a sense of direction and continuity. Main labels establish a sense of context and deepen visitors' understanding. Group labels, captions, and identifications impart specific information about artifacts. Longer labels, like main or group labels, should present the most important information first and begin with specific and concrete details about the objects on view. Something observable but not obvious—a physical property, the origin or use of an object, the significance of a name, a distinctive characteristic—provides a good opening tactic and will lead the reader to ask other questions. The beginning should grab a reader's attention; how you compose the rest of the label's content will determine if you can hold that attention.

Like poems or advertising copy, labels must compress information into a small space at the same time that they hold interest and make the reader want to learn more. A few rules of thumb can help your words serve these ends. Use active verbs and avoid the verb "to be." Write short, crisp sentences and avoid long words. Sentences should average fifteen words; twenty-five is the maximum. Try to stay within range of 130 to 150 syllables per hundred words, and an average of ten to twenty words per sentence. Practice a variety of techniques to add interest as you write draft copy. What questions spark your reader's curiosity? What quotations suggest larger meanings? Can you make comparisons with everyday, modern objects? Do your instructions invite a reader to interact with the exhibit?

Above all, write and rewrite until your labels actively engage your reader. And be prepared to bend and break these rules of thumb.

History by Design

We have surveyed planning a historical exhibit from the space it will occupy to the things it will contain. These elements work together by placing real things into an environment designed to enhance their meaning and suggest their significance. Our discussion focused on the audience to emphasize that exhibits are primarily means of *communication.* Exhibits are designed to encourage intellectual and emotional participation. Once in place, exhibits need to be evaluated to insure that the audience's needs have been met. Plan a period between installation and opening to step back from your work and take an objective and critical look at what you have done. Be willing to make changes. Revision and reflection are as critical to an exhibit's success as the thought, effort, and resources you have invested in preparing it.

The reward for your effort will be the new appreciation of history that lights the faces of visitors, young and old, as they tour your exhibit and leave talking about what they have seen. Exhibits are a particularly rewarding way to create history because exhibits physically embody ideas, present the past with impact, and can give visitors a renewed sense of who they are and how their community came to be.

Conclusion:

CELEBRATING THE
TEXAS SESQUICENTENNIAL

"THE HISTORY OF EVERY COUNTY begins in the heart of a man or a woman," wrote Willa Cather in *O Pioneers!* When Texans celebrate our state's Sesquicentennial, we will be commemorating the rich and diverse experience of men and women who shaped communities all over the state. That heritage will properly give meaning to the Texas Sesquicentennial.

Historical exhibits are only one way to honor our history, but exhibits are also one of the most effective ways to present the story of a community's past and to involve members of a community in it. At the community level, today's Texans will be most intimately involved and personally touched by past events and their commemoration. The Texas Sesquicentennial Commission's *Community Handbook* lists nine different types of exhibits among its project ideas for local planners. This primer has shown how exhibits are created, suggested considerations that need to be addressed, and indicated where you can go for more help.

The traces of the Texas past are as broad and as rich as the experience they signify. In the final analysis, the question is not whether Texans will celebrate their Sesquicentennial but how well we deal with this moment. Like all birthdays, the Texas Sesquicentennial will have a festive and a serious side. It should be an occasion for parades, ceremonies, and other special events. But it is also an opportunity to reflect on our past, to see how we have measured up to our ideals and how far we have yet to go. Because most of us find identity in our immediate environment, we all need to reconsider the meaning and significance of our own local heritage. The history of every community belongs in the hearts of its living members. Sesquicentennial exhibits and programs allow us to put it there.

Notes

❧·❀·❧

Notes to Chapter 1: THINKING HISTORICALLY

This chapter is based on "Where is the Past? The New Community History and Where It Comes From," presented by Don Carleton, Director, Barker Texas History Center, University of Texas at Austin.

(p. 3) Ron Tyler recalled Carl Becker's definition of history for me. It is explored in Becker's presidential address to the American Historical Association, "Everyman His Own Historian," *American Historical Quarterly*, XXXVII (January, 1932), pp. 221–236.

(p. 4) Two excellent explorations of how historians create history are: Barbara Tuchman's *Practicing History: Selected Essays* (New York: Alfred A. Knopf, 1981)—a superb collection of reflections by America's best narrative historian; and, David Hackett Fischer's *Historians' Fallacies: Toward A Logic of Historical Thought* (New York: Harper Torchbooks, 1970)—a delightfully written account of the ways in which historians have drawn conclusions from the evidence.

(p. 6) Kathleen Neils Conzen, "Community Studies, Urban History, and the American Local History," in Michael Kammen, ed., *The Past Before Us: Contemporary Historical Writing in the United States* (Ithaca: Cornell University Press, 1980), pp. 270–291, discusses the traditional local history and the revival of popular and academic interest.

(p. 6) Peter N. Stearns "The New Social History: An Overview," in James B. Gardner and George Rollie Adams, ed., *Ordinary People and Everyday Life: Perspectives on the New Social History* (Nashville: The American Association for State and Local History, 1982), pp. 3–21, provides an overview of the approaches now being explored.

(p. 7) See Kathleen Neils Conzen, "The New Urban History: Defining the Field," in Gardner and Adams, ed., *Ordinary People and Everyday Life*, pp. 67–89.

(p. 7) H. P. R. Finberg's concept of concentric circles is explored in his essay, "Local History," in H. P. R. Finberg, ed., *Approaches to History: A Symposium* (Toronto: University of Toronto Press, 1962), pp. 121–122.

(p. 8) Robert Wiebe, *The Search for Order: 1877–1920* (New York: Hill and

Wanz, 1967) traces how the meaning of community and the character of American communities changed in response to modernization.

Notes to Chapter 2: THINGS SAID AND DONE

This chapter is based on the sources and comments provided in "The Treasure Hunt: Potential Sources for Local History," presented by Patrick Butler, Curator of Collections, Harris County Heritage Soceity, Houston, and Ron Tyler, Assistant Director for Programs and Collections, Amon Carter Museum, Fort Worth.

(p. 20) For a lively discussion of historical evidence and inference, see Allan J. Lichtman and Valerie French, *Historians and the Living Past: The Theory and Practice of Historical Study* (Arlington Heights, Illinois: Harlan Davidson, 1978).

(p. 24–30) For more complete discussions of working with newspapers, public records, city directories and commercial histories, landscapes, maps, and architecture, see especially the following:
   Phillip C. Brooks, *Research in Archives: The Use of Unpublished Primary Sources* (Chicago: University of Chicago Press, 1983).
   David E. Kyvig and Myron A. Marty; *Nearby History: Exploring the Past Around You* (Nashville, Tennessee: American Association for State and Local History, 1982).
   Fay D. Metcalf and Matthew T. Downey, *Using Local History in the Classroom* (Nashville, Tennessee: American Association for State and Local History, 1982).
   David Weitzman, *Underfoot: An Everyday Guide to Exploring the American Past* (New York: Charles Scribner's Sons, 1976).

(p. 27)Paul Boyer and Stephen Nissenbaum, *Salem Possessed: The Social Origins of Witchcraft* (Cambridge: Harvard University Press, 1974). See also, James West Davidson and Mark Hamilton Lytle, *After the Face: The Art of Historical Detection* (New York: Alfred A. Knopf, 1982), p. 28–53.

(p. 31) A sample of how artists portrayed Texas can be found in William H. Goetzmann and Becky Duval Reese, *Texas Images and Visions* (Austin: University of Texas Press, 1983).

(p. 31–34) Three useful introductions to visual materials are:
   Julia Hirsch, *Family Photographs: Content, Meaning, and Effect* (New York: Oxford University Press, 1981).
   Lois Swan Jones, *Art Research Methods and Resources: A Guide to Finding Art Information* (Dubuque, Iowa: Kendall Hunt Publishing Company, 1978).
   Robert A. Weinstein and Larry Booth, *Collection, Use, and Care of Historical Photographs* (Nashville, Tennessee: American Association for State and Local History, 1977).

Notes to Chapter 3: THINGS LEFT BEHIND

This chapter is based on "What is the Past? Using Objects as Historical Sources," a slide presentation by Conover Hunt, museum consultant and former Curator of Collections at the Dallas Historical Society.

(p. 38) James Deetz, *In Small Things Forgotten: The Archaeology of Early American Life* (Garden City, New York: Anchor Books, 1977) explores how recovered objects reveal the history of those who left few written records.

(p. 38) Three excellent collections of essays on material culture—the study of artifacts—are:

Ian M. G. Quimby, ed., *Material Culture and the Study of American Life* (New York: W. W. Norton and Company, 1978).

Thomas J. Schlereth, *Artifacts and the American Past* (Nashville: American Association for State and Local History, 1980).

Thomas J. Schlereth, ed., *Material Culture Studies in America* (Nashville: American Association for State and Local History, 1982).

(p. 39)For a further elaboration of the identity, context, and associations, see Jules David Prown, "Mind in Matter: An Introduction to Material Culture Theory and Method," *Winterthur Portfolio*, Vol. 17, No. 1 (Spring, 1982), pp. 1–19.

(p. 39) for the Colonial Williamsburg Study, see Barbara G. Carson and Cary Carson, "Things Unspoken: Learning Social History from Artifacts," in James B. Gardner and George Rollie Adams, ed., *Ordinary People and Everyday Life: Perspectives on the New Social History* (Nashville: American Association for State and Local History, 1983), pp. 186–190.

(p. 41) Henry Glassie's phrase is quoted in Thomas J. Schlereth, ed., *Material Culture Studies in America* (Nashville: American Association for State and Local History, 1981), p. xvi.

(p. 41) Mary Johnson, "What's in a Butterchurn or a Sadiron? Some Thoughts on Using Artifacts in Social History," *The Public Historian*, Vol. 5, No. 1 (Winter 1983), pp. 61–81, explores how household objects can be keys to broader topics such as the role of women, the development of consumer goods, and the design of house interiors. See John A. Kouwenhoven, *The Arts in Modern American Civilization* (New York: W. W. Norton and Company, 1967), pp. 13–42, for a discussion of how American tools evolved to fit their environment and improved on European designs.

(p. 42) See Barbara Tuchman's essay, "History by the Ounce," in her *Practicing History: Selected Essays*, (New York: Alfred A. Knopf, 1981), pp. 33–45.

(p. 46) The phrase "artifactual ideas" is used in H. J. Swinney, "Introductory Essay," in Arminta Neal, *Exhibits for the Small Museum: A Handbook* (Nashville: American Association for State and Local History, 1967), pp. 1–8.

Notes to Chapter 4: CREATING HISTORY BY DESIGN

This chapter is based on "Turning Lead into Gold: How to Synthesize Research into Exhibits," slide presentations by Sam Hoyle, Director of the U.S. Army Air Defense Artillery Museum, Fort Bliss, and David Ross, Director of the McAllen International Museum.

(p. 53) Two other sources on exhibit design are: R. S. Miles et al, eds., *The Design of Educational Exhibits* (Boston: George Allen and Unwin, 1982) which reflects the authors' experience in planning and producing exhibitions for the British Museum (Natural History), includes an extensive bibliography, and represents the most complete discussion of educational exhibits in print; and,

James Gardner and Caroline Heller, *Exhibition and Display* (New York: F. W. Dodge Corporation, 1960) which focuses on trade shows and merchandizing products, but also disucsses many considerations applicable to museum exhibits.

Appendix:

RESOURCES FOR TEXAS COMMUNITY HISTORY

Compiled by Patrick H. Butler, Curator of Collections,
Harris County Heritage Society, Houston

I. ARCHIVES

The institutions included in the following list represent many of the major centers for archival collections in Texas. Usually, these collections focus beyond the immediate community in terms of the range of materials available. There are many fine county archives which would be consulted by and known to individuals engaged in research within a particular community. I would like to express appreciation to Nancy Parker, the Special Collections Librarian of the Woodson Research Center of the Fondern Library at Rice University.

ALPINE
  Sul Ross State Unviersity
  Byron Wildenthal Memorial Library
  Archives of the Big Bend
  Alpine, Texas 79830
  915-837-3461, ex. 271
AMARILLO
  Amarillo Public Library
  Local History Collection and John L.
    McCarty Papers
  Box 2171
  Amarillo, Texas 79105
  806-372-4211, ex. 264
ARLINGTON
  University of Texas at Arlington
    Library
  Department of Special Collections
  P.O. Box 19218
  Arlington, Texas 76019
  817-273-3391
AUSTIN
  Austin Public Library
  Austin-Travis County Collection
  P.O. Box 2287

Austin, Texas 78767
512-472-5433, ex. 35

Catholic Archives of Texas
P.O. Box 13327
Capitol Station
Austin, Texas 78711
512-476-4888

Daughters of the Republic of
  Texas, Inc.
Museum
112 East 11th Street
Austin, Texas 78701
512-477-1822

Lyndon Baines Johnson Library
2313 Red River
Austin, Texas 78705
512-482-5136

Texas State Library
Archives Division
P.O. Box 12927
Capitol Station
Austin, Texas 78711
512-475-2445

University of Texas at Austin
E. C. Barker Texas History Center
Austin, Texas 78711
512-471-5961

University of Texas at Austin
Nettie Lee Benson Latin American
    Collection
Austin, Texas 78712
512-471-3818

CANYON

Panhandle-Plains Historical Museum
Library and Archives
P.O. Box 967
W. T. Station
Canyon, Texas 79106
806-655-2567

COLLEGE STATION

Texas A&M University
University Archives and Manuscripts
    Collection
College Station, Texas 77843

COMMERCE

East Texas State University
Library
University Archives
Commerce, Texas 75428
214-468-3162

CROSBYTON

Crosby County Pioneer Museum
P.O. Box 386
Crosbyton, Texas 79322
806-675-2331

DALLAS

Dallas Historical Society
Research Center Library and Archives
P.O. Box 26038
Dallas, Texas 75226
214-421-5136

Dallas Public Library
1954 Commerce Street
Dallas, Texas 75201
214-749-4100

Southern Methodist University
DeGolyer Library
P.O. Box 399
S. M. U. Station
Dallas, Texas 75275
214-692-2661

Southern Methodist University
Perkins School of Theology
Methodist Historical Library

Dallas, Texas 75275
214-692-3496

EDINBURG

Pan American University Center
Library
Special Collections
Edinburg, Texas 78539
512-381-2754

EL PASO

El Paso Public Library
Southwest Collection
501 N. Oregon
El Paso, Texas 79901
915-543-3815

University of Texas at El Paso
Library
Special Collections
El Paso, Texas 79968
915-747-5697

FORT WORTH

Amon Carter Museum
Photography Collections
P.O. Box 2365
Fort Worth, Texas 76101
817-738-1933

Fort Worth Public Library
Local History and Genealogy
    Department
9th and Throckmorton
Fort Worth, Texas 76102
817-870-7740

National Archives and Records Service
Federal Archives and Records Center
Archives Branch
P.O. Box 6886
Fort Worth, Texas 76115
817-334-5515

Southwestern Baptist Theological
    Seminary
Fleming Library
P.O. Box 22000–2E
Fort Worth, Texas 76122
817-923-1921, ex. 277

GALVESTON

Rosenberg Library
Archives Department
2310 Sealy
Galveston, Texas 77550
409-763-8854

University of Texas Medical Branch
Moody Medical Library

Department of Archives and
  Manuscripts
Galveston, Texas 77550
713-765-1971

HOUSTON

Harris County Heritage Society
1100 Bagby
Houston, Texas 77002
713-223-8367

Houston Public Library
Houston Metropolitan Research Center
500 McKinney
Houston, Texas 77002
713-222-4900

Rice University
Fondren Library
Woodson Research Center
P.O. Box 1892
Houston, Texas 77001
713-527-8101, ex. 2586

Texas Gulf Coast Historical Association
University of Houston Library
Houston, Texas 77004
713-749-2727

Texas Southern University
Library
Heartman Negro Collection
3201 Wheeler
Houston, Texas 77004
713-527-7148

KINGSVILLE

Texas A & I University
John E. Conner Museum
P.O. Box 2172
Station 1
Kingsville, Texas 78363
512-595-2819

LA PORTE

San Jacinto Battleground Museum
3800 Park Road–1836
La Porte, Texas 77571
713-479-2421

LIBERTY

Sam Houston Regional Library and
  Research Center
P.O. Box 989
Liberty, Texas 77575
409-336-7097

LUBBOCK

Texas Tech University
Southwest Collection

P.O. Box 4090
Lubbock, Texas 79409
806-742-3749

NACOGDOCHES

Stephen F. Austin State Unviersity
Ralph W. Steen Library
Special Collections Department
P.O. Box 3055
SFASU Station
Nacogdoches, Texas 75961
409-569-4101

PLAINVIEW

Wayland Baptist College
Van Howeling Memorial Library
Caprock-Plains Historical Collection
1900 W. 7th
Plainview, Texas 79702
806-296-5521

SAN ANTONIO

Archdiocese of San Antonio
Catholic Archives at San Antonio
P.O. Box 32648
San Antonio, Texas 78284
512-344-2331

Bexar County Archives
Office of the County Clerk
San Antonio, Texas 78205

Daughters of the Republic of Texas
Library
The Alamo
P.O. Box 2599
San Antonio, Texas 78299
512-225-1071

San Antonio Public Library
203 St. Mary's Street
San Antonio, Texas 78205
512-223-6851, ex. 42

University of Texas at San Antonio
John Peace Library
Special Collections
San Antonio, Texas 78285
512-691-4570

SAN MARCOS

Southwest Texas State Unviersity
Library
Special Collections
San Marcos, Texas 78666
512-245-2191

TEXARKANA

Texarkana Historical Society and
  Museum

P.O. Box 2343
Texarkana, Texas 75501
214-793-4831
WACO
Baylor University
Library
P.O. Box 6307
Waco, Texas 76706
WASHINGTON
Star of the Republic Museum

Washington State Historic Park
P.O. Box 317
Washington, Texas 77880
409-878-2461
WICHITA FALLS
Midwestern State University
Moffett Library
3400 Taft Street
Wichita Falls, Texas 76308
817-692-6611, ex. 204

For further research on the resources in Texas archival collections, the following volumes will be of help

National Historical Publications and Records Commission. *Directory of Archives and Manuscript Repositories.* Washington, D.C.: National Archives and Records Service, 1978.

Day, James M. *Handbook of Texas Archival and Manuscript Depositories.* Austin: Texas Library and Historical Commission, 1966.

II. MUSEUMS

The following list includes a number of museums with staff and collections which might serve as resources for research on local Texas history projects with a material culture emphasis. Museums on this list are larger history museums. Certainly many county museums also have resources which should be tapped.

ALPINE
Museum of the Big Bend
Sul Ross State University
Alpine, Texas 79830
915-837-3461, ex. 212
AUSTIN
Daughters of the Republic of Texas
Museum
112 E. 11th Street
Austin, Texas 78703
512-477-1822
Texas Memorial Museum
2400 Trinity
Austin, Texas 78712
512-471-1604
CANYON
Panhandle-Plains Historical Museum
P.O. Box 967

Canyon, Texas 79016
806-655-7191

CORPUS CHRISTI
Corpus Christi Museum
1919 North Water Street
Corpus Christi, Texas 78401
512-883-2862
DALLAS
Dallas Historical Society
Hall of State
State Fair Grounds
P.O. Box 26038
Dallas, Texas 75226
214-421-5136
Old City Park
1717 Gano Street
Dallas, Texas 75215
214-421-5141

EL PASO
El Paso Centennial Museum
UT El Paso
El Paso, Texas 79968
915-747-5565

FORT WORTH
Amon Carter Museum
P.O. Box 2365
Fort Worth, Texas 76101
817-738-1933

Fort Worth Museum of Science and
History
1501 Montgomery Street
Fort Worth, Texas 76107
817-732-1631

GALVESTON
Rosenberg Library
2310 Sealy
Galveston, Texas 77550
409-763-8854

HOUSTON
Harris County Heritage Society
1100 Bagby
Houston, Texas 77002
713-223-8367

Houston Museum of Fine Arts
P.O. Box 6826
Houston, Texas 77005
713-526-1361

KINGSVILLE
John E. Conner Museum
Box 2172, Station 1

Kingsville, Texas 78363
512-595-2819

LA PORTE
San Jacinto Museum of History
3800 Park Road–1836
La Porte, Texas 77571
713-479-2421

LUBBOCK
The Museum
Texas Tech University
P.O. Box 4499
Lubbock, Texas 79409
806-742-2428

MIDLAND
Permian Basin Petroleum Museum
1500 Interstate 20 West
Midland, Texas 79701
915-683-4403

SAN ANTONIO
Institute of Texan Cultures
P.O. Box 1226
San Antonio, Texas 78924
512-226-7651

Witte Memorial
3801 Broadway
San Antonio, Texas 78209
512-826-0647

WASHINGTON
Star of the Republic Museum
P.O. Box 317
Washington, Texas 77880
409-878-2461

III. REGIONAL HISTORICAL RESOURCE DEPOSITORIES

Persons whose names are starred (*) are Texas State Library staff members stationed at Depositories. Others are staff of house institutions where no TSL staff member is stationed.

ANGELO STATE UNIVERSITY
Joe B. Lee, Head Librarian
Angelo State University
San Angelo, Texas 76909
915-942-2222

AUSTIN PUBLIC LIBRARY
Audray Bateman, Curator
Austin Travis County Collection

Austin Public Library
P.O. Box 2287
Austin, Texas 78768
512-472-5433, ex. 282

BAYLOR UNIVERSITY
Kent Keeth, Director
Texas Collection
Baylor University

Box 6896
Waco, Texas 76706
817-755-1268
Reference Contact: Virginia Ming

DALLAS PUBLIC LIBRARY
Wayne Gray, Head
Texas Dallas History & Archives
  Division
Dallas Public Library
1515 Young St. 7th Floor
Dallas, Texas 75201
214-749-4151
Reference contact:
  Mary Lynn Rice-Lively,
  Interlibrary Loan
  214-749-4347

EAST TEXAS STATE UNIVERSITY
James H. Conrad, University Archivist
James G. Gee Library
East Texas State University
Commerce, Texas 75428
214-886-5737

HOUSTON PUBLIC LIBRARY
*Ribert Schaadt, Field Archivist
RHRD & Local Records Division
Texas State Library
Houston Metropolitan Research
Houston Public Library
500 McKinney Avenue
Houston, Texas 77002
713-224-5442, ex. 340

MIDWESTERN STATE UNIVERSITY
Melba Harvill
Director of Libraries
Midwestern State University
Wichita Falls, Texas 76308
817-692-6611, ex. 4165

NORTH TEXAS STATE UNIVERSITY
Richard Himmel, University Archives
A. M. Willis, Jr., Library
North Texas State University
Box 5188, NTSU Station
Denton, Texas 76203
817-788-2411, ex. 239

PAN AMERICAN UNIVERSITY
George Gause
Special Collections Library
Pan American Library
Edinburg, Texas 78539
512-381-2799

PARIS JUNIOR COLLEGE
Lulane Carraway, Librarian
Learning Resource Center
Paris Junior College
Paris, Texas 75460
214-785-7661, ext. 215

SAM HOUSTON REGIONAL LIBRARY
& RESEARCH CENTER
*Robert Schaadt, Director & Field
  Archivist
Sam Houston Regional Library &
  Research Center
P.O. Box 989
Liberty, Texas 77575
409-336-7097

SAM HOUSTON STATE UNIVERSITY
Charles L. Dwyer
Special Collections
Sam Houston State University
Huntsville, Texas 77340
409-294-1619

SHERMAN PUBLIC LIBRARY
Hope Waller
Library Director
Sherman Public Library
421 N. Travis St.
Sherman, Texas 75090
214-892-4545, ex. 240

STEPHEN F. AUSTIN STATE
UNIVERSITY
Linda Nicklas
Special Collections Librarian
Stephen F. Austin State University
Box 13055, SFA Station
Nacogdoches, Texas 75962
409-569-4101

TARLETON STATE UNIVERSITY
Dr. Kenneth W. Jones
University Librarian
Tarleton State University
Stephenville, Texas 76402
817-968-9246
Reference contact:
  Harvey Gover, Public Services
  Librarian

TEXAS A & I UNIVERSITY
Mrs. Jimmie Picquet
John E. Conner Museum
Texas A & I University
Kingsville, Texas 78363
512-595-2819

TEXAS A & M UNIVERSITY
  *Paul R. Scott, Field Archivist
  University Archives
  Texas A & M University
  College Station, Texas 77843
  409-845-1815
TEXAS CHRISTIAN UNIVERSITY
  *Nancy M. Merz, Regional Supervisor
  Library
  Texas Christian University
  Fort Worth, Texas 76129
  817-921-7106
TEXAS TECH UNIVERSITY
  Kathryn Lewis, Librarian
  Special Collections
  Texas Tech University
  Lubbock, Texas 79409
  806-742-2242
  Reference contact:
    Gloria Lyerla, Reference-
    Interlibrary Loans
TEXAS STATE LIBRARY
  *Wendie Brown-Hill
  Regional Historical Resource
    Depositories & Local Records
    Division
  P.O. Box 12927
  Austin, Texas 78711
  512-475-2449
UNIVERSITY OF TEXAS AT DALLAS
  Larry Sall, Assistant Director for
    Special Collections
  University of Texas at Dallas
  Box 643 MC 3.3
  Richardson, Texas 75080
  214-690-2570

UNIVERSITY OF TEXAS AT EL PASO
  Cesar Caballero, Head
  Special Collections Department
  University of Texas at El Paso
  El Paso, Texas 79968
  915-747-5697
UNIVERSITY OF TEXAS AT PERMIAN
BASIN
  Bobbie Klepper, Research Assistant
  Learning Resources Center
  University of Texas at Permian Basin
  Odessa, Texas 79762
  915-367-2128
VICTORIA COLLEGE
  Virginia Allen, Government Documents
    & Archives Librarian
  VC–UHVC Library
  2602 North Ben Jordan
  Victoria, Texas 77901
  512-576-3151, ex. 201
WEST TEXAS STATE UNIVERSITY
  Claire R. Kuehn
  Archivist-Librarian
  Panhandle-Plains Historical Museum
  Box 967, WT Station
  Canyon, Texas 79016
  806-655-7191, ex. 8

COUNTIES WITH NO DESIGNATED
DEPOSITORY
  *Carmela Leal, Field Archivist
  G. J. Sutton Building
  321 Center Street
  Room B–031
  San Antonio, Texas 78202
  512-226-5926